TACKLE LIFE
HEAD ON

A PLAYBOOK ON
DEFEATING LIFE'S OBSTACLES

JEFF OGDEN

TACKLE LIFE HEAD ON

A Playbook on Defeating Life's Obstacles

Book Design by Transcendent Publishing
www.transcendentpublishing.com

Author Photography by GODOYSHOTS Photography Studio, Farmers Branch, TX

ISBN: 978-0-578-32527-9

Disclaimer: This book is designed to provide motivation to our readers. It is not intended as a substitute for professional medical advice or emergency treatment. Do not use this information to diagnose or develop a treatment plan for a health problem or disease. If you're in a life-threatening or emergency medical situation, seek medical assistance immediately.

Printed in the United States of America.

DEDICATION

For my baby girl – I wouldn't change a thing
because it all led to you.

Pointing to Peytan after scoring a TD in preseason.

TABLE OF CONTENTS

INTRODUCTION

I decided to write this book because I knew I had a story that everyone could relate to. I felt my experiences could serve as inspiration for others who are facing adversity and looking for tools to address them. During our lifetime, we have all faced obstacles and challenges we had to overcome. As you will soon learn, I am no stranger to obstacles – from childhood disabilities and the rigors of playing football in the NFL, to a life-threatening car crash and learning to live with a devastating brain diagnosis, which continues to this day. Though these situations differ vastly from one another, they had two things in common. The first was that the odds were definitely *not* in my favor. The second was that the challenges, no matter how difficult, were not as determinative of the outcome as my own efforts, feelings and beliefs. My commitment to these truths, along with guidance from God and loved ones, led me to develop an expanded vision about my capabilities and the belief that I could accomplish the impossible.

In the pages that follow, you will read many anecdotes from my life, from the embarrassing and absurd to the tragic. While many reference football, the heart of the story is how I, a regular kid from a small town, was able to dismiss the doubters and negativity while maintaining my focus on my dreams. This meant deciding at an early age that I wouldn't live according to the many labels or diagnoses ("too sickly," "too small," "too slow," and "permanently disabled, to name a few) that were placed on me and instead turn my "disabilities" into "capabilities." My chosen occupation, while pretty unique, also taught me a great deal. Football, as they say, is a metaphor for life, and from it I learned that miracles happen when we refuse to stop working, trusting, and believing. One degree, one workout, one catch, one-tenth of a second, one repetition, one habit, made my miracle happen and allowed my dream to become possible.

This book is intended to serve as a catalyst for your self-exploration and growth. How you use it is up to you. You can read it cover to cover, skip to more relevant chapters, or work through the "Timeouts" – just be sure to take your time and take notes. Committing your goals to paper helps you to envision them clearly in your mind – both the desired outcome and the incremental steps you need to reach them. It may also show you that some of the obstacles looming large in your mind actually have a straightforward solution. Whatever you choose, my sincere desire is that you will realize that with faith, hard work, and a sense of humor, you will be able to conquer any obstacle Head On!

PRE-SEASON

This section speaks to struggles I experienced growing up, each of which helped set the groundwork for my future. Every NFL player has had obstacles in their lives that they had to overcome, much the same as any parent, student, business professional, and so on does. I'm not saying that I had more than my share, but I'm betting they're much different from most! Indeed, from the way my life started, I would never have believed I could have a five-year career as a professional football player.

DRAFT DAY

My family, agent and I - about ten of us in total – gathered around our landline phone that hung in our modest kitchen and dining room. We were so intent on waiting for it to ring that when it did, in the late seventh round of the 1998 NFL draft, we were actually startled. I began fielding calls, as did my agent. One after another, the call-waiting feature alerted me to potential team prospects. In total, around fifteen teams called, and like car salesmen tried to sell me on the opportunity I would have with their organization. Only this "dealership" offered incentives in the form of signing bonuses. Signing bonuses are the only guaranteed money for the prospects. While bonuses in this modern area are in the tens of millions, I couldn't be happier with the five- or six-thousand-dollar bonus I was offered. After a twenty-minute frenzy, I, at twenty-two years old, had to make a decision that would potentially impact the entirety of my future. Needless to say, the energy was palpable, with my crowd members sitting at the edge of their seats in anticipation of the final decision. I finally hung up the phone and in a daze told them that I had just agreed to a contract with "America's Team"...The Dallas Cowboys. At once, there was an eruption of cheering, joy, and tears. With goose bumps and tears in my eyes, I embraced my mom and dad... a feeling that I had grown dependent on throughout my senior year of football in college. It was a surreal moment, and the realization of a goal that had once seemed like nothing more than a pipedream.

Holding my niece, Mackenzie, on the phone with the Dallas Cowboys on draft day, 1998.

Right now you may be asking yourself, *So what? Why is this a big deal?* Well, it's because the story leading up to receiving that phone call to play professional football was not a typical one; in fact, it was full of obstacles, difficulties and challenges that are very unique. Let's dive into why playing in the NFL seemed like a "miraculous" accomplishment.

"LOOK, MOM, NO LEGS!"

"Everyone around us began to scream!" my mom recalled of the moment my lower leg appeared to fall off onto the floor. I was two years old at the time.

My mom, sister, and I were at a grocery store. My three-year-old sister Janelle walked alongside our cart while I sat in the child's seat up top. I was dangling and swinging my legs back and forth, and the motion caused one of my casts to slip off my foot and fall to the ground. Janelle calmly told Mom that "Jeffy's leg just fell off," and apparently other shoppers overheard her, saw my cast on the ground, and gasped in horror. I thought it was great. My leg was still attached obviously, and I was ready to begin living my life without any hindrances …or so I thought!

Most of us spend little time appreciating the miracle of our bodies – from breathing to walking to allowing us to experience the world through our five senses. It's only when our bodies begin to "fail" us that we realize how much they do for us every minute of every day. As someone who has faced physical limitations basically from birth, I know what an enormous obstacle this is. Sometimes we can overcome them, sometimes we must find ways to work around them, but there is always a way to find joy and purpose in our lives – by drawing strength from our faith, our families, and our abilities to help others.

While I was still in my mother's womb, the doctors were able to see that there was an abnormality with my feet – they were curled in tight little balls and would not straighten on their own. This variation of clubfoot needed to be treated as soon as I was born. The first treatment consisted of placing casts on both of my feet in an attempt to elongate them and prevent my ankles from turning in further. My mom has told me that I seemed okay with them on my feet. The tubes in my ears, however, were another story. I had constant infections and was not responding to sound. Concerned about permanent damage to my hearing, my doctors admitted me to the hospital for a week of treatment, including the insertion of the ear tubes. It was during that stay that I spoke my first word. From the hospital bed, I looked out the window and said, "Bird." I guess I figured that since I couldn't walk, maybe I'd just fly like he did!

That was just the beginning. In fact, during the first two years of my life I spent more time at the hospital than at home, being pumped with "pediatric cocktails" to treat my asthma, eczema, and hearing. Indeed, the clubfoot was the least of my worries.

I was a pleasant and happy but hyperactive child, according to my mom. I couldn't wait to get my casts off, so I learned to walk with them on. She remembers my legs began growing abnormally strong as I had to carry the weight of the casts around with me. Once they came off, I was forced to wear corrective open-toed boots with a metal bar that kept my feet separated. (When she told me this story, all I could picture was Forrest Gump. Ha!) I only had to wear the braces at night, which freed me up to walk normally during the day. My "normal," though, consisted of me walking and running everywhere on my tiptoes. Later, my gait remained abnormal as I would walk toe-heal instead of heal-toe. I was an awkward child in middle school – "ballet walking" down the hallways at school and wheezing from asthma. It's no surprise that I didn't have a girlfriend!

In middle school, I began experiencing even more health conditions. My asthma was under control with a steady dose of pills and breathing treatments, but I had debilitating migraines. I would get several a year, and they always seemed to develop at the worst and most stressful times – when I had an important test at school, competing in sports, or planning to hang out with friends in loud environments. I never knew when they might occur or how to prevent them, and the uncertainty kept me from enjoying a normal childhood. With each migraine, I would experience excruciating pain in my head and eyes, accompanied by nausea. My parents would have to drive me to the emergency room, where I'd get a shot and a warm towel over my eyes before returning home to sleep it off. Maybe those of you over twenty-one can relate. Ha!

FATHER KNOWS BEST

I've often been asked at what age I started playing football. The answer surprises most as I had a relatively late start compared to other professional football players. While I began playing organized football in the eighth grade, about fourteen or so, I had been in love with the game since the age of nine. My dad was an all-around athlete who excelled at several sports, including football; he even had a chance at a tryout with the Chicago Bears. His greatest strength was kicking, and on many occasions,

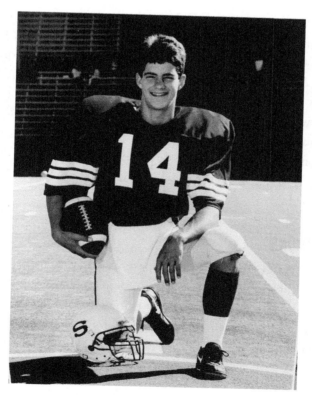

Senior year of High School, 157 lbs.

he would let me tag along as he punted ball after ball into orbit. Looking upward and with my puny arms outstretched, I would shuffle left and right in an attempt to position myself under the ball's path. There was that sense of suspended time as I eyeballed its trajectory; then, assuming I was lucky enough to be in the right spot, I'd attempt to catch it. More often than not, the ball would smack down upon my forearms before it fell to the grass. Dad would call out to me, saying, "It's okay, you can let it hit the ground first and then throw it back to me." This may have sounded like he was letting me off the hook – far from it.

It was a challenge of sorts, one he knew would drive me to work harder and become more determined. And it worked; in time, I learned to shift my focus from the pain (and the blistering welts that resulted) to my goal of catching every football my dad could punt. Years later, I would draw on those practice sessions when I stood on the NFL field, waiting for the ball to fall from the sky as eleven men with bad intentions sprinted toward me. As a kid, I didn't have any grown-ass men aiming at running through my chest, but the stakes seemed the same to me. I channeled the focus I was fortunate enough to develop at nine years old each time I stepped onto an NFL field. I have my dad to thank for instilling the intangibles necessary to be successful at the highest level. I just wish he would've at least mentioned those big scary men who would be chasing me one day. Ha!

NFL PREDICTIONS

Most people recall something their parents said while they were growing up – a philosophy or heartfelt statement that will forever stand out in their minds. For me, one of those things was my dad's early prediction that I would one day play professional football, which, given all the physical challenges I faced, was pretty amazing.

When I've talked with other players and heard about their journey to the NFL, it always seemed they were destined for greatness at an early age; for me, however, nothing could be further from the truth. As a kid, football was just another sport in my long list of athletic endeavors that included soccer, baseball, track and basketball. Then, around age ten, I was drawn into another sport: gymnastics. This new challenge would require a level of commitment that would lay the foundation for my NFL career.

My neighbor, who was a few years older than me, was involved with gymnastics at that time. I knew nothing about it but thought it was cool that he could flip around the yard. I had to give it a try. Over the next several years, I excelled, becoming a three-time Illinois State Champion and Junior Olympian. To achieve this, I had to practice six or seven days per week. On a typical day I would leave school, eat dinner in the car, and train for two or three hours. Always my biggest fan and supporter, my dad chauffeured me back and forth and sat behind the spectator's glass, eyes glued to my every move.

During the competitions, before I even saluted the officials to begin my programmed routine, I would glance over to my parents. My dad would point to his head, then his biceps (he was a powerlifter, so his arms were hard to miss), before placing his two index fingers on top and to the side of his head. This form of sign language communicated three things: Think... Strong... like a Water Buffalo! I laugh as I write this now, but having his familiar face and his unwavering support meant the world to me. I was fortunate to have a lot of success in gymnastics, but the highlight of every competition was his hug after the competition. He accepted that thankless role and asked nothing in return. Or so I thought...

My first years of football, in junior high school, provided nothing to write about in this book. Simply put, they involved me getting out-muscled, out-skilled, and out-played. I was a senior in high school before I earned a starting spot as the quarterback. Once that happened my dad began planting seeds that I could one day play in the NFL. To me, nothing seemed further from the realm of possibilities. Just five-foot-nine and one hundred and fifty-seven pounds, I had a lot of practice reps under my belt but next to no experience playing in games; nevertheless, my dad insisted that I could one day suit up in the NFL. Following my senior year I didn't receive an ounce of interest from any of the hundreds of collegiate football programs, I thought surely my dad's fantasy would be put to rest. It was not. Even when I spent a few years warming the bench as a walk-on for a small university, he continued to believe that if I got a chance to play, I would excel and go on to play professionally! I was completely convinced, well, 99.9% convinced, that he had lost his mind...as was everyone else in my family. Yet Dad never wavered – not as the events of my senior season in college played out, or through the draft, the training camps, and, finally, making an NFL roster. He didn't just believe I would play in the NFL, he *knew* I would. I owe so much to my dad, and have failed so many times to show him how grateful I am. I did make good on the one thing, the *only* thing he ever asked for in return: a hat. But he didn't want just any old hat, but the kind players and staff wore on the sidelines. He now has a closet full of limited-edition hats, and that doesn't begin to express my love and gratitude for him.

ACTUAL PSYCHIC PREDICTION

Each week, several of my Dallas Cowboys teammates met for an evening Bible study. On this particular week, one of the guys invited a psychic to speak with us. We all sat around a player's living room staring at her – some with arms crossed in disbelief and some questioning *her* beliefs. And then there was me, the twenty-three-old rookie, sitting amongst older and wiser teammates with an innocent smile on my face. I was about to witness a Christian psychic speak. I was intrigued and excited.

I was in for a lot more than I expected that evening. After a half-hour of casual chitchat, she began to look around the room. Then, sporting something between a smirk and a grin, she would turn to one of the players and very pointedly, make prolonged eye contact with him before predicting their future. As she went around the room I grew more nervous, knowing my turn would soon come.

The psychic spoke about other players' pasts, and their future professional and family prospects. She spoke about the blessings they would have in their communities and in their lives after football. Finally, her eyes locked onto mine and her perma-smirk widened into a full-blown smile. Her eyes sparkling, she relaxed back into her chair and in her New Orleans drawl asked, "What's your name, hon?"

With trepidation, I answered her. She then began to shake her head slowly from side to side, seemingly listening to God give her my life's resume. "God is giving me the word *peculiar;* I feel like you're 'Mr. Peculiar.'" My face flushed with embarrassment as my teammates began to grin in agreement. "You're not like these other boys, are you? You whistle your own tune... you don't feel like you fit in, do you?"

Now she had my attention. Maybe she wasn't a quack. Maybe she *did* have God's ear. Or, maybe I just looked out of place around these other elite physical specimens, ha. She spoke for a few more minutes about things I can no longer remember, then announced that she had a "vision."

"Hon, God is showing me an image of a father hovering over a baby boy who is first learning to walk. The baby boy is excited, and trying to run without any assistance or fear. He is confident knowing his daddy is right there to catch him if he falls. You are that boy, Mr. Peculiar. God has His hands hovering above you. You will break records, and God will smile down on you and always be there to catch you when you fall."

Okay, she is a quack! I thought. *I'm a rookie, ecstatic just to be on the team, and this "microphone for God" thinks that I'll set records in the NFL?!* I left the Bible study thinking more about HOW she knew I was "peculiar" than the eventual records I was destined to collect.

I can now look back with an equally big smile as that psychic had that evening. She was right. I did set records. But what I remember most of all was that I was free to run as fast as I could, knowing that God would always catch me if I fell. Throughout my life, I would put Him to that test and He has always made good on His promise!

Now, let's get back to some more obstacles.

PERFECTION IS MY ENEMY

I know there are a lot of mistakes in this next paragraph, but my guess is you'll be able to understand it, even with the imperfections.

I've always vued "Perfection" as an endgame, destination, chalenge, or gole. I felt it was the measure of my eforts, weather it be in athletics, relashunships, faith, or work. I beleeved that if I worked hard enough, I would be rewarded with the word of affirmation, I so deeplee desired. Once agin, I was rong.

Oh, relax! I warned you there'd be a lot of mistakes in that last paragraph. (It drove my editor crazy to leave them!) Yet I'd be willing to bet you understood it anyway. I achieved my "communication goal," therefore, it can be said that the paragraph was perfect.

Now imagine you had taken one look at the paragraph and dismissed it as nonsensical or too difficult to read. You would have missed the message, and possibly an opportunity to learn something of value. Looking back, I can see now that perfectionism was, in fact, an obstacle in my life. This fantasy began when I was a child gymnast, then rippled out to my faith, health and fitness, football, and my careers.

In gymnastics, I was judged on a scale between 1 and 10. Every gymnast's goal was to have a perfect score, of course, and I dedicated many hours, days, and months to achieving that magical two-digit number. I surrendered control of my happiness and self-worth to a group of judges who would determine if I was "perfect." Today, I cannot remember how many perfect scores I received, but I can clearly recall the routines for which I scored a 9.9. It was torture for me to know that the smallest

Guess I only played sports that require tight pants!

error, such as a bent toe, robbed me of that precious tenth of a point. It also took most of the joy away from the sport and brought about stress, anxiety, and illness to an otherwise happy childhood.

A "sin" is an archer's term that means the arrow has missed the bulls-eye. It signifies an imperfect shot. I mistakenly adopted that mentality as it pertained to my relationship with God. I would become overwhelmed with guilt if I lived an imperfect life in any way. I remember feeling so guilty about walking past a wrapper lying on the ground on my college campus. After my friends and I were about twenty yards beyond the wrapper, my conscience kicked in and I ran back to deposit it into a trash receptacle. I am not perfect, and I later understood that God knew that and loved me, perfectly anyway.

Due to my lifelong involvement in athletics, nutrition and exercise have always played a big role. I, however, took it to an unhealthy level; I had to be perfect. I couldn't eat a healthy meal and "reward" myself with a dessert, as that would be counterproductive, a failure in my eyes. I had a black-and-white mindset when it came to nutrition: it was either perfect, or horrible. The same mentality applied to how I trained and conditioned my body. I felt the more I trained, the better I'd perform. In fact, I was doing my body a disservice by not allowing muscles to rest and recover.

For professional football players, keeping their job has a direct correlation to how they perform on Sundays. Over the course of my five-year career, this meant a constant fear of being cut each Monday. Each time I ran out on that field I felt I had to perform perfectly so as not to be cut in favor of another, more perfect player. While this was based in some reality, it was an awful way to approach the game I loved. My insatiable appetite for perfection was stealing the joy of having achieved my dream.

Winston Churchill said, "Perfection is the enemy of progress." Seeking out the unrealistic goal of perfection can cause us to shy away from opportunities and steal our joy in life. Models in magazines, filtered photos on social media, a perfect gymnastics routine, never dropping a ball, and never eating a piece of cake is not reality. Mistakes happen. Accept them, learn from them, and move on. I say "eat your cake and work out too!" I don't think Churchill would have put it quite that way, but I'm pretty sure it's what he meant.

VIEW FROM MY DAD'S HUG

Though there is a lot of love in my family, we are not a particularly demonstrative bunch. Out of us four kids, I received the most attention, which of course, I felt was justified! Ha. Partly this was because I was the baby of the family, but mostly it was because I was so sickly and needed the extra care. I needed my mom to rub my head after I received my shots for my migraines. I needed my dad to carry me up the stairs to bed because my asthma wouldn't allow me to climb them. I needed both of them to calm me down after my night terrors sent me running out of the house at night. They did this, without fail, for years. As I said, though they did not always display affection, I never questioned their love.

THE FIRST TRIMESTER … I THINK I'M PREGNANT

Disclaimer: Ladies, forgive me for my comparison of birthing my work ethic to the beauty of the childbearing process. In no way, shape or form does anything in my or any other man's life remotely hold a candle to the mental, emotional, and physical challenges y'all endure during those nine months, while in labor, and for the rest of your lives. My level of admiration and respect for you is incomparable to that of anything else I've ever accomplished. Every one of you deserves your names in the record books, a bronze bust (hee-hee), and a helmet for the days you want to bang your head against the wall. On behalf of all men on the face of this earth, we love you and we're sorry. I will forgo my urge to compare my drive to be the best with your cravings for pickles and peanut butter. I'll also refrain from comparing the fans and reporters screaming for my attention to the children screaming for their mothers. And in no way will I state that the physical pain I felt after a game was the same as childbirth – promise! If you haven't yet thrown this book in the garbage, please read on… it's a humbling chapter!

JUST A BABY PEANUT

Growing up, I was what some would call a "wimpy" boy. (See, I told you it was humbling!) I was quick, coordinated and strong, but I seemed to be half the size of the other kids my age and was routinely made aware of that fact. I recall one particular incident that happened in the sixth grade. During history class, I was misbehaving and distracting the other students. My teacher quieted the entire class down, then his attention turned to me. "Jeff, what do you think you're gonna do with your life?" Though I was just seventy-five pounds and "masculinely petite" for my age, I possessed a much larger man's confidence. Knowing that I had the full attention of the class, I arrogantly responded, "I'm gonna play in the NFL!" The class chuckled. Not amused, my teacher continued in a more aggressive tone. "You're not even starting on our junior high team… you're too slow… and too small… you'll *never* play in the NFL!" That embarrassed me, not just because I didn't have a snarky comeback, but because I believed him. For some reason, I have never forgotten those words spoken to me as a twelve-year-old, nearly three decades ago. (Don't do the math; I'm only thirty-six!)

I do not hold anything against my history teacher. I was disrupting his class and making his job more difficult. And since I had mentioned an unrealistic goal of playing football in the NFL, he probably felt taking me down a peg (or several) was a way he could capture my attention and reel in my behavior. I wish I could say he was alone in that sentiment, but others would convey a similar one, often when I had done nothing to provoke them.

A similar exchange occurred when I told the track coach at my community college that I was transferring to Eastern Washington University to try out for the football team. Without mincing any words, he told me that I would never go as far in football as I would as a pole vaulter. He had plans for me to be the first American to vault over the twenty-foot threshold. (As of February 2021, 19 feet, 10.5 inches is still the American record.)

During that same time period at community college, I worked for a family pizza restaurant as a dishwasher. With excitement, I gave my two weeks' notice and explained that I would be giving football a try at the collegiate level. The owner, sizing me up, echoed the words of my history teacher and track coach. "You'll get killed," he said, shaking his head from side to side. Nearly twenty years later, I was back in Oregon to watch my nieces play in a summer basketball tournament. Of course I had to take them back to that restaurant (and not only because I loved their pizza, but because I had ulterior motives). After ordering, I was disappointed to learn the owner wasn't in yet – then, halfway through our pizza, I saw him walk through the door. "Hey! "It's Jeff Ogden," I said, genuinely pleased to see him. I could tell he had to jog his memory a bit. Then he asked me what I had been up to since leaving Oregon for Cheney, Washington. I gladly (and humbly, wink, wink) filled him in, thinking this was a teachable life-lesson moment for my nieces. I now know that it was prideful of me, that what I really wanted was to see the look on his face when he realized I had proven him wrong. Instead, he congratulated me on my success and showed me pictures of his grand-kids. My pride immediately dissipated and I felt like a jerk.

These situations in my earlier years would serve as great motivators moving forward. Those "doubters'" words kept me in the weight room longer and inspired me to condition harder in the off-season. The words they spoke birthed in me a passion and a strong desire to be the best football player I could be. At that time, I believed making a college football team was the apex and that convincing the coaches to let me play was my biggest obstacle. Looking back, I understand that my obstacle was to overcome the words of others and believe in myself.

TIMEOUT: TAKING THE NEXT STEP

"Understand that you cannot apply equal energy to everything. Be conscious of your immediate goals and operate accordingly."

~Ally Love

In everything I try, my goal is never to be "the best." That mentality gives away too much control. I cannot control the scores of games, or the skill levels of others. Even if I'm crowned the victor, I still may not have performed as well as I could have. Instead, I am always determined to reach my greatest potential. As a child with crippled feet and asthma, my potential may not have been as high as other future NFL football players. It was with this in my mind that I worked as hard as I possibly could to maximize my talents and overcome the physical limitations that I was dealt at an early age. I imagined my ultimate goal being at the top of a staircase, with each stair representing a smaller, intermediate goal. My focus would then be on doing everything within my control to take that next step, knowing it led to my ultimate goal of reaching the top of the staircase.

CHALK TALK

Write down a very specific goal, then break it down into five intermediate steps/goals that will help you arrive at the top of your staircase. Now, briefly write down what you'll need to climb that first step. This can be overcoming outer obstacles, such as a physical challenge, or inner obstacles, such as a lack of belief in yourself.

_____

_____

_____

_____

_____

_____

_____

_____

_____

_____

_____

_____

_____

SECOND TRIMESTER: BIG BROTHER IS CALLING

My brother Pat was the reason I received a second chance to play football. After receiving zero interest from any of the *seven-hundred and sixty-eight* football programs in the United States, I walked onto the track team at Clackamas Community College. I spent the fall and winter training as a pole vaulter and truly enjoyed it. I was also making great gains, as my sole focus, other than academics, was on track and field.

That fall season was a season of firsts. One, I was living away from home for the first time; two, I was teammates with a female pole vaulter. Those realities turned out to be no big deal. My family was only three and a half hours away, and I was so busy I didn't have much time to feel lonely. My teammate was an amazing athlete and, as females had historically not participated in this event, a trailblazer as well. It was change number three during those first six months of college that was the most difficult to deal with: not playing football.

Since track was going so well, I never expressed to anyone my sadness about this noticeable void in my life. After classes and track practice, I would try to content myself by watching any football I could find on TV – back then there weren't any streaming services; no YouTube, Google, Hulu, ESPN+, et cetera. One Thursday evening, as I sat on my bed, my remote control found a football game on one of the six available stations. No matter that it was a local junior high team – I focused intently on every play. I don't know what specifically triggered me, but at some point during the game, my eyes began to fill up with tears. I grew angry with God and asked Him to remove this passion of mine…to allow me to move on from this pipedream… to ease my pain... but felt He wasn't listening. I missed the game of football more than ever.

Two months later, in January 1994, my brother called to chat. Again, at this time no one knew of the struggles I was going through concerning my desire to play football. I only spoke of the progress I was making in the classroom and on the track.

During the conversation, Pat asked me, "How would you like to be an Eagle?"

Dumbfounded, I responded, "Wait!… What?… How?"

"How would you like to come up to Eastern and play football?"

"Are you serious?!" I asked, now pacing around my apartment.

"Yeah, I went in and met with the new coach and he agreed to let you come up and try out for this spring. Then they'll evaluate your ability."

Without hesitation I interrupted, "Yes, yes, a million times, yes!!" (Well, I didn't really say it that way, but I'm pretty sure that's how dramatic I felt.)

My brother was a bit of a legend at Eastern Washington University during his time playing Strong Safety on the Eagles' defense. He was known for his aggressiveness and hard-hitting abilities. His teammates have told me that when the ball was snapped, his eyes would grow wide and fill with red. At times, he would find himself out of proper position but made up for it with his speed and bone-bruising tackles.

My "playing style" was the polar opposite of Pat's, as was my body type. His legs, hips, and thighs were massive, but he had trouble doing any push-ups. ⊠ I, on the other hand, had long legs and a strong upper body. He was built for hunting down Running Backs and Receivers, and I was built to avoid defensive players like him.

Our mentalities matched our physical make-up. He went full speed on everything athletically. He was either in fifth gear or in park – nothing in between. I, however, floated through gears when it benefited me most. Fifth gear was reserved for running away from defenders like my brother.

He did not possess the "fight or flight" response, only a "fight or fight harder" response! In the course of my career, I would witness similar mentalities in only a few other players – my teammates Zach Thomas (Linebacker for the Miami Dolphins); Ray Lewis (Linebacker for the Baltimore Ravens); and Ed Reed (Safety for Baltimore Ravens) are amongst them. Mike Singletary (Chicago Bears) and Lawrence Taylor (New York Giants) were a couple that I remember watching on TV growing up. Just like Pat, these players' eyes told the story. Before each snap, they seemed to enter a hyper-focused state. They were football machines with the intent to cause severe damage. Though my brother did not play at the NFL level, his mindset equaled the players I mentioned, all of whom are considered amongst the best of all time.

Needless to say, my brother's phone call was an answer to my private prayers.

A few weeks before the spring semester begun, I moved up to Spokane, Washington and enrolled at EWU. As I was not on scholarship and didn't receive a housing allowance, I lived with Pat about forty-five minutes from campus. My introduction to college football began with a team meeting. I did not know a soul, and I don't remember anything about the meeting, other than following the herd to lunch afterward. Upon showing up to the cafeteria, everyone scanned their scholarship cards and received a food tray. (Since I was a walk-on, I didn't have a food allowance either.) Eventually, I would become friends with a freshman quarterback Harry Leons, who was also a walk-on. His parents provided him with a meal plan, and for the next few years, he allowed me to share in some of their goodwill. But for that first meal I had to pony up the cash.

After lunch, I made my way to the equipment room to checkout my football gear. Due to four stress fractures in my back that were sustained in high school, I was required to wear rib and back protector pads, which fit like a bulky corset. My cleats were black, heavy high-tops. Underneath my right cleat I wore a plastic ankle brace because of torn ligaments I had sustained playing basketball just ten weeks prior. Then the equipment personnel asked me what jersey number the coaches assigned me to wear.

"Eighty-three," I replied.

Wrong answer. Immediately, they informed me that eighty-three belonged to Tony Brooks, a record-breaking receiver who was dominant his entire collegiate career. Though he was a senior and his career at Eastern was over, I apparently wasn't considered worthy of wearing his jersey number. I didn't blame them, though, and when they handed me a number eighty-eight jersey I walked away humbled, and very grateful.

I suited up for my first collegiate practice as a wide receiver – a position I had never played before. (I played quarterback in high school.) Even if I had played receiver back then, it would have been an understatement to say I did not look the part. There I stood – all five-foot-ten, one hundred and seventy pounds of me – with my helmet and oversized shoulder pads that connected to my rib protectors. My football pants held my hip, butt, thigh and kneepads. My clunky high-top cleats and ankle brace supported my steps. My gear weighed nearly as much as I did. I felt like the little boy in *A Christmas Story* when his mom bundles him in a million layers before sending him on his way to school in the snow. When that little boy fell, he couldn't stand back up due to all his jackets, and I could only hope I wouldn't suffer that same fate!

But none of that mattered – not the weight of the gear, or the jersey number, or the price of school lunches. My dream was taking shape. God, who I'd accused of ignoring me just months earlier, had a plan, and He had used my brother Pat to deliver the opportunity. Now, however, the responsibility rested on my shoulders right along with my bulky football pads. If I were to continue living out the dream I would have to make a name for myself that spring and prove I could contribute to the team.

TIMEOUT #2: ATHLETIC SUPPORTER

Doubt had a way of rearing its head at some of the most crucial times of my life – especially during my football career. Would I start on the varsity football team in high school? Would any college allow me to play for them? Would I ever see the collegiate field? Would I get a chance to play professionally… and would I make a roster?

Looking back, I found confidence through my family and support system. My family provided the cheerleading that gave me the strength to press on. Doubt can feel powerful in the moment, but when opposed by unwavering love and support of those closest to you, it gains no stronghold.

CHALK TALK

Who is your support system? Do they know how they can best support you and your dreams/goals? Is there anything or anyone that could potentially hold you back? Write down the names of those in your current support system. Write a brief summary of what you need from them, be it an action on your behalf or just listening to your concerns or challenges, then speak to each of them individually and communicate those needs.

ME, A HEISMAN HOPEFUL?!

The Spring Football Camp at EWU consisted of practices, film review, playbook study, and a total of three team intrasquad games. I was a season behind and felt way in over my head. All my teammates, who already had at least one season under their belts, were fluent in the language of offensive schemes and terminology – a language I had never learned. In our receiver meetings, we would discuss the various defensive coverages. Our Offensive Coordinator spoke of Will, Mike, and Sam. I believed those were the names of my linebacker teammates. It wasn't until a week into spring camp that I learned they were actually general terms used to describe the specific linebacker's position. Will=Weak-side Linebacker. Mike=Middle Linebacker. Sam= Strong-side Linebacker. As I said, I was in *way* over my head.

Though I tried my best to minimize that steep learning curve, I never fully grasped my position, my route terminology, or our offensive schemes. I was one of fifteen receivers and last on our depth chart. Fortunately, in spring intrasquad games, everyone would have a chance to play.

After a week of practices, we had our first intrasquad game. Our first and second-string offense would play; only then, after they had played a majority of the scrimmage, would the third- and fourth-stringers get their chance. In the fourth quarter, I was instructed to get in the game. After our Quarterback called the play we broke from the huddle. Still not having a complete understanding of my role, I lined up at the receiver position. I was relieved that it was a running play and that my job was simple: block the defender in front of me. And that's what I started to do as soon as the ball was snapped. As I ran out to meet the defender, I looked back and saw the running back racing toward me with a linebacker in hot pursuit of him. Instinctually, I left my defender and sprinted toward the defender chasing down our running back. He didn't see me until right before I drove my shoulder pads and helmet into his chest, knocking him off his feet. He laid on the ground, holding his ribs and gasping for air while the rest of his defensive team-mates yelled at him to get back up. Exhilarated, I walked back to the huddle, where I received a bunch of chest bumps and slaps on my butt for my effort. Little did anyone know that I was also seeing stars. I did my best to hide my distress. Later in the game, I caught four passes for over one hundred yards and scored two touchdowns. The next day I was shocked to see my name in the newspaper, but my eyes literally grew wide when I saw, in a small paragraph next to the main article, the words "Heisman Hopeful." (The Heisman Trophy is awarded to the best player in college football each year.) Those words were actually said in response to a question from a reporter, who had asked our Head Coach to comment on my performance in the game. Coach Kramer responded jokingly, "We found our Heisman Hopeful!"

It seemed like the start of a running joke when the reporter again asked about my performance after our second scrimmage, in which I produced similar results. Perhaps slightly annoyed, Coach offered this dismissive response: "Oggie is progressing well, but has a long way to go in the process of becoming a productive receiver for our team. He is putting up great stats, but those catches and touchdowns are against our third- and fourth-stringers." Some guys might have been discouraged by his comments – I just thought it was cool to see my name in the paper, not once, but twice!

We had one more scrimmage – the annual Alumni Spring Lobster Feast and Red & White Game. Unlike the prior two, there would be a lot of fanfare. We would be suiting up in our game uniforms and have fans, cheerleaders, and referees. It was a game-like situation and the score mattered.

I didn't see any action against the first- or even second-string defense; however, my production in the previous two scrimmages had earned me the opportunity to play a majority of the second half. I took full advantage.

Since I still didn't have a complete understanding of our offense, the wide receiver's coach would yell out to me the route I needed to run. I ended up catching seven passes during the game, three of which ended in touchdowns. This made the reporters even happier than the coaches. The next day, my name was more than just "mentioned"; I grabbed the main headline on the front page of the sports section! Was I a Heisman Hopeful? Of course not. But for a brief moment that spring, I felt like one.

That first experience with collegiate football was a whirlwind. I overcame a new environment, new playbook, new position, a bulky football uniform and, most importantly, a limited budget for food! My efforts were recognized by the coaches, and I was awarded a partial scholarship that covered my tuition for the following year. Though I was incredibly grateful for the opportunity to live out my dream of playing college football, the actual playing wouldn't come so easy. Let's just say I became very familiar with the bench area, and the cheerleader's dance routines! Ha.

MY THIRD TRIMESTER: BIG BROTHER IS WATCHING

"Today, I'm going to give it my 'some'!"

My brother's on-the-field intensity carried over to his off-the-field training regimen. It was during our summer workouts that he helped develop my work ethic. I possessed some talent and skills, but it was my determination and physical and mental preparedness that would separate me from other players in the future. I took great pride in this area because it was an aspect of football that I was in complete control over. I believed that if I was in superior shape, I could gain an advantage with how hard I hustled. To do that, I would have to train harder than anyone else in the off-season.

After the game and this photo, my brother made me run more sprints! Ha.

Pat knew and believed this as well. My asthma would be my biggest adversary in my attempt to be the most physically fit. Running and breathing were not my strong suits, and they were crucial to my position as a wide receiver. This obstacle reared its head all too often growing up; in fact, I'd used my asthma as an excuse as to why I couldn't perform well in sports. Though Pat knew it was partially true, he had no pity. Instead, he consistently reminded me that because of my asthma I would have to train twice as hard just to level the playing field. His "no excuses" mentality didn't just help me get into better physical condition, it also laid the groundwork for the mindset I needed to possess throughout my career in the NFL and beyond.

As we headed into summer break, our strength and conditioning coach provided each player a booklet filled with workouts to complete. The weightlifting portion provided every exercise, every repetition, and weight to be lifted. The cardio-conditioning workouts consisted of specific sprinting drills. The summer workout booklet also included distances to be run, target times to hit, and the number of sprints to complete. It was a very detailed and specific outline that would physically prepare us for the upcoming fall season. My brother was able to read the outlines as well as I could, but he interpreted them much differently. He felt the expectation of the Strength & Conditioning program was merely a "suggestion"… for those who only wanted to do the bare minimum. It certainly wouldn't suffice for me, someone who was already operating at a disadvantage and needed to train harder than everyone else. He increased my number of sprints and cut down the length of time I had to rest between them. Ninety-degree days are not uncommon throughout Spokane summers, and it was not uncommon for me to vomit during the course of these training sessions.

"Throwing up makes you look weak, Jeff!" Pat would yell. "Don't let anyone see you look tired!"

On days when I had to work out on my own, he expected me to account for my reps, sprint times, and rest times; he also asked me how many times I had thrown up. I'm not sure if it was a healthy goal of mine to not vomit, but I soon mastered it. That newly acquired skill of keeping my food down paid off for me many times in the NFL during our two-minute drills on national TV! Ha.

Even on my days "off," Pat was relentless. He would take me to an isolated area north of Spokane, where his friend owned a few acres. It provided the best and most grueling training one could imagine, including Beatty Mountain, which had a very steep incline. Pat would set up cones on the rough path up the hill, then we would sprint from cone to cone up the hill without stopping. Pat, then twenty-seven, was still in excellent shape. If I weren't able to keep up with him, I was forced to pay a penalty as he resorted back to his playing days. Crouching down around twenty yards from me up the hill, he'd tell me I had to avoid him or he would "throw" me. He wasn't lying. On my first attempt to sprint up the hill I did everything I could to avoid his grasp. I failed, and all two-hundred-ten pounds of muscle smashed into me and flung me onto the dirt. Angry, embarrassed, and in pain, I stood up and with tears in my eyes and finished my sprint up the hill.

I didn't drastically improve my cardiovascular conditioning with that final sprint up the hill. I did, however, drastically improve my toughness and will to fight, which was my brother's ultimate goal. Well done, Pat – now take me to Golden Corral for the all-you-can-eat buffet (our favorite post-workout indulgence)!

FAILING TO MAKE WEIGHT

Weight was always an issue for me growing up, especially when it came to football. I was very slim and matured later than other boys my age. Even when I began to grow, it was only vertically – no matter how much I consumed, I couldn't put on a pound. My lunches in high school consisted of several sandwiches, snacks, and a can of syrupy pears that I had to ask the cafeteria staff to open for me. In addition, nearly every day of my senior year, I would walk to our neighborhood grocery store during a break. For around two dollars, I could buy a box of six Hostess raspberry-filled powdered donuts – plus two "bonus" donuts included! I would devour all eight and still my body fat and weight never changed – a problem that no longer exists, by the way!

I spent my summers in high school five hours away from home at Pat's house, where I was able to focus all my time and energy on preparing for the upcoming football season. Pat had his own methods of trying to help me gain weight – some bordered on the extreme and were certainly disgusting. I remember eating piles of spaghetti for lunch, dinner, and nighttime snack, and mixing up "Mega Mass 2000" protein shakes to drink twice per day. At the time I was working as a parking lot attendant at a children's amusement park, and it was nothing for me to eat six to eight sandwiches during a shift. But the worst "meal" by far was consumed during a fishing trip on the lake. We weren't catching anything so Pat promised me a pair of his used running shoes if I ate some of the fish bait. I was seventeen years old, impressionable, and wanting to impress my big brother. I put the grub worms in my mouth, showed them to him on my tongue, chewed, and swallowed. It was a win-win. I got a few extra calories and a pair of Nike running shoes. I later found out that my mom gave him money in exchange for those shoes. Oh Well!

It wasn't until my junior year of college that I grew into my full frame, standing six-foot-one and 185-pounds. My nutrition (which no longer included eight donuts), combined with my incessant desire to train, allowed me to reach my full physical potential at that time. I had waited out the obstacle of gaining healthy weight and now, at twenty-two, finally started to see my strength and size catch up to other Division-1 football players. The progress was encouraging and further fueled my desire to work harder. It paid off. I finally earned a full scholarship going into my junior year. This meant I received a housing stipend and cafeteria allowance. Although I would still graduate with school debt, this helped out tremendously and I was extremely grateful. I had also participated on EWU's track and field team, for which I was awarded a book stipend. It was a small bread-crumb, but I ate it with pleasure.

SENIOR YEAR OF COLLEGE

Heading into my senior year of football eligibility, I was not slated to be a full-time starter but would be sharing repetitions/playing time with a fellow senior wide receiver. I recall being okay with that role, and did everything I could to prepare leading up to the season. I had filled out physically and was in the best shape of my life. My dream of playing

Papa was happy even after driving to Arizona to watch me play.

and making a difference on a college football team was taking shape. My coaches were going to give me the opportunity to play on the same field my brother had just eight years earlier. Four years had passed since that fateful call from Pat, yet it was never far from my thoughts. At this time, football was still joyful and stress-free. I developed close friendships with my teammates and played for them as much as for myself. Thinking this was the last football season of my life, I didn't have any personal goals heading into that season other than to play, contribute to victories, and have fun.

My family had their own goals for that year, which included traveling five hours over Snoqualmie Pass to watch our home games. My dad's goal was to drive to *every* game my senior year, even as far as Flagstaff, Arizona. He succeeded. My entire family would show up to my games adorned in Eastern Eagles football gear from head to toe. They would wave pom-poms and whatever else our marketing department gave away on gameday. Knowing that they were in the stands provided me much-needed support in college and later in the NFL.

Our team goal was very simple: we wanted to win our first outright Conference Championship. We played at the Division 1-AA (now called the FCS) level. It's a lower tier than the bigger schools that are televised on Saturdays, so we were happy if the local news came out to cover our game and interview us. The most dominant teams in our conference were the Idaho Vandals and Montana Grizzlies. Idaho had just moved up to Division 1-A, the highest level in college football, but remained on our schedule. The Grizzlies entered the 1997 season as the number-one team in the nation. These two rival games would be pivotal if we were to have a chance at achieving our goal to be The Big Sky Conference champions and they proved to be pivotal for my future career in the NFL.

PRANK CALLS WITH MY QUARTERBACK

My best friend and quarterback was hilarious; you would consider yourself lucky to get a straight answer out of him, about anything. We hung out the night before every game, each pretending to be the coach as we delivered the pre-game speech to a group of invisible players. Though we used Coach's favorite phrases, a majority of the speeches had nothing to do with football at all, and they never failed to elicit laughter. On the day before our first game, we had the bright idea to call in to the local radio show that covered all the college sports programs in the area. Our football program was rarely spoken of or covered, but we were going to remedy that. We created a script that contained a few talking points, then I called in using an alias. When the host introduced me, "Ebru," to his listeners. I announced myself as a huge fan of the Eagles football team, and then tried to generate some excitement around our upcoming year by boasting of our high-powered and explosive offense and the toughness of our defense.. I had no idea what I was talking about or even if we could make good on my promises. Fortunately, our team did.

WELL-SEASONED

Our first game of the 1997 season came against Rocky Mountain College. My first catch of the season ended in a touchdown. I went on to score three touchdowns in the first half. I sat out the second half as our team rolled to a 63-7 victory. Eastern Oregon traveled to our stadium in Cheney, Washington for the second game of the season. In similar fashion, I scored my fourth, fifth, and sixth touchdown before I sat out the second half of that game. We began the season with two convincing wins and I was able to solidify a starting position. I no longer had to share plays with anyone else.

The stage was set for me, not only to live out my dream of playing college football, but to actually do it well. As a team, we were trending in the right direction. We found ourselves undefeated after our first four games heading out to Bozeman, Montana to face the Montana State Bobcats. During that game, our quarterback sustained a concussion early in the game and we suffered our first, and only, regular season loss. We went on to defeat every opponent on our way to the first Big Sky Conference Championship.

TWO BIGGEST GAMES OF THE YEAR

Montana Grizzlies

We were bussed out to Missoula, Montana to meet up with the number-one ranked team in the nation. They also with thirty-five straight victories, possessed the nation's longest home winning streak at the Division-1 level. The twenty-thousand-seat stadium was located in a picturesque area, surrounded by mountains so close it seemed like they were right on top of the playing field. Later, I would recall this field when I saw Lambeau Field, home of the Green Bay Packers, as they provided a similar atmosphere for players and fans alike.

It was a beautiful fall day for the sold-out crowd. Before we exited, our Head Coach approached me and the other receivers. He told us that we would win this game if we were able to block well for our running backs. While this wasn't very exciting for me to hear, I planned on blocking my butt off if it meant a win over the mighty Grizzlies.

The game didn't play out as expected. I'm pretty sure I was more shocked than our coaches. We found ourselves in a shootout with the Grizzlies' high-powered offense. The game began with my main role to serve as a blocker. Fortunately, I was able to contribute more. I'm unable to remember the catches, but I ended the game with three touchdowns, a two-point conversion catch, and over two hundred yards receiving. More importantly, we dethroned the kings of the conference. It was after this game that I, and everyone else, knew our team was going to be special. We had gained traction and were building momentum.

After another victory the following week, we prepared to take on the other bullies of the Big Sky Conference: the Idaho Vandals. That game would take place at a much larger venue that could accommodate the crowd expected for this rivalry competition: Joe Albi Stadium in nearby Spokane.

Idaho Vandals

The air in the stadium on that chilly November afternoon was nothing short of electric. Our rivalry with the University of Idaho, which was seventy-one miles away, dated back decades, and the Vandals always seemed to win the recruiting wars. Year after year, they put out great teams that competed for championships. As mentioned, the Vandals had moved up to Division 1-A for the 1997 season but remained on our schedule. For us, it presented an opportunity to compete against a larger school that had more scholarship players on their roster.

At this time, myself and Harry Leons, our quarterback and a fellow walk-on, had moved past the stigma of unproven players. We had both experienced success that year and were on pace to set several single-season records, so we were both especially looking forward to our face-off with the Vandals. Certainly, it was something we would remember for the rest of our lives…or not in my case.

With the exception of the last two minutes I recall nothing of that game, and Harry has corrected me about what occurred during that short time span. I even had to google our stats. So, really, I only remember one thing: waking up after being knocked unconscious.

"DON'T WORRY, I WON'T HURT YOU."

– Harry Leons

Spectators of football may have a pretty good idea of what is happening after a team breaks out of their huddle and approaches the line of scrimmage. However, I'd like to share an interesting viewpoint of when I broke the huddle in college.

Harry, being my best friend and quarterback, felt pretty comfortable with putting my health at risk! Ha. I would always joke about passes he threw during games that could potentially lead to me taking a big hit by the defense. I also thought I was open at all times. This was a constant, ongoing conversation that most QBs and receivers have throughout the season. To this day, we still discuss games, throws, and blame each other for poor plays or lost games.

When a certain play is called, the QB has an idea of where he should be throwing the ball. Harry when presented with equal options, would inevitably choose to throw my direction. He knew that if he didn't he wouldn't hear the end of it from me the following week. When our offense was down within the five-yard line against Idaho, we broke the huddle. While the rest of the offense jogged up to the line of scrimmage, Harry grabbed the shoulder of my jersey and said, "Don't worry, I won't hurt you!" This was not an isolated occurrence and it offered no consolation, but to his credit he did not hurt me on that particular touchdown pass. Later in the game, he didn't make the same claim before throwing the pass that got me knocked out. I guess he never lied though, ha.

After battling with Idaho the entire afternoon, we were losing by five points with around two minutes left in the fourth quarter. However, we also had the ball and therefore a chance at victory. All the Vandals had to do was keep us from scoring a touchdown and they'd head back to Moscow, Idaho with a win. The philosophy of defenses in these situations is to play back deep to prevent any big plays. Essentially, the job of Idaho's safeties was to keep everything and everybody in front of them, and they played it almost perfectly... almost.

Not surprisingly, Harry was under intense pressure during those last two minutes of the game. As they had all year, our offensive line protected Harry as if he was their newborn baby. This allotment of time allowed him to throw a tight spiral over the middle of the field. After I caught the pass and with adrenaline pumping, I sprinted to the nearest sideline, got out of bounds, and stopped the clock. The following play called for me to run a deep post route. This meant that I was to sprint down the field aiming for the goal post. The offensive line came through once again, giving Harry enough time to heave the ball down the field in my direction. As the ball began falling down toward my arms, I knew there was a free safety running over to put a big hit on me in an attempt to break up the completion. I leaped up, stretched out my arms, and snatched the ball out of the air. At that moment, the Vandal's safety ran through the back of my ankles. I was upended and came down onto the old-school artificial turf. The back of my head hit first and I "went to sleep."

I woke up on the 1-yard line with one minute left on the clock. The first thing I remember is the training staff huddled around and on top of me.

"Oggie, can you move your legs?!" the head trainer asked.

"Did I catch the ball?" I responded.

"Can you squeeze my hand?" one of the staff asked with urgency in his voice.

"Did I catch it?" I said, matching their intensity.

"Yes Oggie, you caught it!"

"Then I'm okay."

I was then escorted off to the sidelines with the training staff's arms holding me up. They packed my helmet away, signifying I would not be returning to the game. I remember shaking off some of the cobwebs and looking out onto the field as our team huddled up. We were on the

1-yard line with less than a minute to play in the game. Suddenly, in a confused state of mind, I began screaming at anyone who would listen.

"Where's my helmet?! I need my helmet!" I cried out, not understanding why I wasn't in the game during this crucial moment.

The staff tried to calm me down and explain what had just happened to me a few minutes prior.

I broke away from their grips and told another teammate to give me his helmet as I was desperate to get back on the field. As he handed it to me, I was again corralled by the training staff and restrained. I then took a knee and looked on angrily and with tears in my eyes. On the very next play our running back took the ball straight up the middle for the game-winning touchdown. I was elated for the victory and so thankful to our amazing training staff who prevented me from further damage to my brain.

THE END OF MY COLLEGE SEASON...AND PERHAPS CAREER?

"Notice who is in the locker room after you lose,
not after you win."

~Angelo Dundee

Our 1997 Eastern Washington University Eagle football team finished 12-2 – a school record for most wins in a season. We also accomplished our goal of finishing as Big Sky Champions for the first time in school history, and several players earned All-American awards. Accolades fell upon our offense, defense, and special teams alike – and deservedly so. Our coaching staff had assembled a team that was among the best in the nation. Unfortunately, our season ended prematurely in the semi-finals when everything went wrong, which was out of character for us. I remember crying in the locker room after that game, though none of those tears had anything to do with the game itself. I was sad that I would never play with my teammates again and perhaps football as well. Just a few months prior, I'd hoped I would get a chance to play. Now I was part of the most accomplished team our university had ever seen.

I had walked onto the field as a freshman wearing bulky shoulder pads, rib protectors, and black high-top cleats. As a senior, I walked off the field with memories of a season I'd never forget, no matter how many concussions I would sustain over the next five years.

PRE-DRAFT SCOUTING EXPERIENCE (DO I FEEL A DRAFT?)

Since my story is very unique, many people have asked me when I knew I had a chance at the NFL. I don't hesitate even for a second, because I can recall that shocking moment like it was yesterday. It was the middle of my senior year at Eastern, following our game against Montana, when an athletic trainer told me an NFL team came to our school to inquire about me. Before my senior season, I hadn't had much playing experience, so I didn't show up on any NFL team's "watch list"; now, after we'd defeated the nation's number-one-ranked team – and I scored on four different occasions – scouts began to take notice. From what I heard, they mainly had questions about who the heck I was. College athletes are not permitted to have any conversations with any NFL personnel until their season is completed. That left the scouts to speak with coaches and watch films of my performance in previous games and seasons, which was very minimal.

My pre-draft workouts began after our season during the winter break. Most of the time, I felt like a steer at a cattle auction. Very methodically, the scouts would measure and test everything. Teams that competed in the colder climates (the Packers, Bears, Chiefs, and so on) were particularly interested in the size of my hands and width of my shoulders. I assume those particular teams were more attracted to tall and heavier receivers. Following the measurement portion, teams would time me in the forty-yard dash. This was the most challenging due to the amount of snow that falls in Cheney during the winter months. Other testing consisted of broad jumps, short and long shuttle, bench press, and vertical jumps. My All-American quarterback, Harry Leons, joined me for the route-running portion. The scout would ask us to run a series of routes and catch passes as he took notes. The New York Jets also administered a psychological evaluation – the only team to do so in addition to the physical tests.

I believe I performed, measured, and tested well enough to garner some interest for potential NFL suitors. The most memorable workout occurred with the Dallas Cowboys. Harry and I seemed to be on the same, perfect page. The scout had us complete several routes and pass catches, which neither of us had ever run and surprisingly handled with ease. It was surreal – four years earlier we had been lowly walk-ons, and now we were demonstrating our talent and skill for the Dallas Cowboys.

PSYCH!

After my senior year in college, NFL teams would stop in at my college to conduct a more personal evaluation of me. As mentioned, for the Jets that included a psychological evaluation. These exams rivaled any I had taken during the course of my college education. After an hour and a half I nervously handed over my exam, then made my way to the athletics fieldhouse to go through a typical pre-draft Wide Receiver's workout. I crushed it! What do you know – the Jets were among just a few teams that did not reach out to me on draft day. I surmised that my psychological examination didn't meet their standards... and that caught my attention more than any other team, even those that *did* call me, ha.

FIRST HALF

"You don't have to love the work. You just have to crave the result so intensely that the work is irrelevant."

~ Unknown

This section, the longest in the book, details the moments from when I signed my first NFL contract to the moment I made the team. I describe my mindset, that of just another kid from a small town, living out a fairytale in which I'm the main character. It contains a lot of details and obstacles you may not know about the daily grind in the NFL, and also a lot of emotion, pain, exhilaration, and of course, more embarrassing stories.

TIMEOUT- LEGACY BLUEPRINTS

Playing for the NFL was no longer a goal...in fact, it wasn't even on my radar. I wanted, and planned on, a career teaching Special Education and coaching at the high school level. I did love football, though, and wanted to play as long as I possibly could. I created a plan to attain that goal as well. Throughout my life my goals have continued to evolve. Life has thrown me a lot of curveballs or, better yet, a lot of wobbly spirals. It has also presented me with many opportunities and blessings. Whatever the circumstances, my eyes had to remain focused on my goals while working diligently through the plans. A great quote I remind myself of often is, "If you are satisfied with your performance, the improvement has stopped." And I choose to remain unsatisfied.

CHALK TALK

How do you want to be remembered? What do you want your legacy to be? What can you do right now, today, to begin to form that? What adjustments, what more can you do, what can you speed up, how else can you develop, back-fill your perceived weaknesses?

Pick a goal or dream and write a paragraph about how you achieved it from the perspective of your future self, ten years from now.

_____

_____

_____

_____

_____

_____

_____

_____

_____

_____

_____

_____

_____

_____

_____

_____

WHY I CHOSE THE COWBOYS

Several factors played into why I chose the Dallas Cowboys during the 1998 NFL Draft. While it was a calculated decision, I had no idea if it would actually benefit me in the end. I even turned down a MUCH larger signing bonus, so I had better be right!

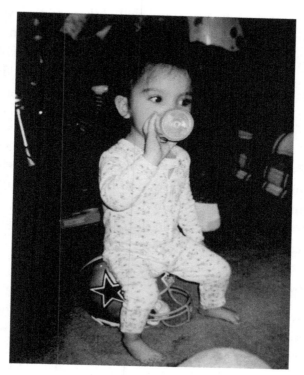

Got my seat.. got my drink.. let's go Cowboys!

THROWING MONEY OUT THE WINDOW

Okay, so it wasn't a huge sum of money, ha. The Seattle Seahawks offered me a six-thousand-dollar signing bonus – the largest I was offered and, for me, an enormous sum of money. Yet that wasn't the biggest draw. I felt signing with my hometown team would make an excellent "feel-good story." Just eight months prior to the April NFL Draft, I had been working as a security guard for the Seahawks during their fall training camp, which was held at my alma mater, Eastern Washington University. I, along with several fellow EWU football teammates, secured the locker rooms, walkways, and sidelines as the team practiced. In truth, we provided little protection for the behemoths adorned in protective covering or the gazelle-like players that were capable of outrunning my Honda Civic. I remember staring, in awe, at the size, speed, and skill of these men, never dreaming that less than a year later I would be invited to join them. After all, I had barely seen the field at my relatively small university. Following the Seahawk's practice, my future All-American Quarterback, Harry Leons, and I served as facilitators for the small children playing a game of touch football that more closely resembled the Puppy Bowl.

I decided to turn down the Seahawks' contract offer and signing bonus. While it was very tempting to play for my favorite team, I felt that I may have too many off-the-field distractions. I needed an environment where I could completely focus on my job. During the upcoming fall season, I would be attempting to play within the chalked lines instead of working to secure them.

LEVEL PLAYING FIELD

Heading into the 1998 season, my rookie year, the Dallas Cowboys hired a new coach, Chan Gailey, who would be introducing his new intricate offense. This came as a relief to me for two reasons. First, I was going to have roughly the same amount of time to study and learn the new offense as the other veterans on the team. Second, I felt Coach Gailey's offensive scheme would drastically increase my chances of making the roster. In the era in which I played, a majority of teams still highly relied on fullbacks – strong, tough, hard-nosed running backs whose primary responsibility was to lead the way for the more agile, glorified running backs. Teams also, for the most part, kept only four receivers on their active rosters. Coach Gailey's offensive scheme, however, at times, would require five receivers on the field at the same time.

LONE STAR PRIDE

The lone star on the Cowboys helmet is much more than decorative – it is symbolic of a pride that runs nearly two centuries deep. Texas gained independence from Mexico in 1836 and became the Republic of Texas. In the process a flag was constructed from a local woman's gown; it bore the lone star above a cannon with the words "Come and Take It" beneath. This phrase, which refers to a cannon that was fought over during the Texas Revolution, has been uttered by Texans ever since.

To this day, Texas flies its own flag at the same level as our nation's flag. It also has its own Pledge of Allegiance, which is recited at schools and events right along with the United States pledge. Indeed, there is no shortage of pride – and, some would say, a slight arrogance – that's displayed whenever anyone or anything attempts to "mess with Texas."

When a Dallas Cowboy slides that helmet onto his head, he carries every bit of that pride with him. When lined up across from an opponent, the player agrees to represent values and traditions that were established centuries before. Anyone who lays a challenge at a Cowboy player's feet will likely be taunted with "Come and take it!"

INSTANT REPLAY: NOT IN OUR HOUSE

In 2000, Terrell Owens, who was playing for the San Francisco 49ers, attempted to celebrate his touchdown by posing on the star on the fifty-yard line at Texas Stadium – according to Cowboys fans, a major act of disrespect. Within seconds, Owens found himself flat on the ground after Cowboy Free Safety George Teague sprinted fifty yards and barreled through him. To this day, I have not seen anyone try that again.

I've also experienced churches that change their Sunday service schedule in the fall to allow enough time for the congregation to get home before the noon kickoff. During the season, "Putting on your Sunday's best" for many consists of pants and a Cowboy's jersey representing their favorite player. Faith, Family, Football are deeply instilled from a very young age, and remain true throughout a Texan's life.

Texas pride is not only strong; it is contagious. I know, because I caught it. Having the opportunity to run out of the tunnel at Texas Stadium bearing that star on my helmet was the ultimate – and seemingly unattainable – dream.

TAKING FLIGHT...DESTINATION DALLAS

Just a few weeks after being signed as an undrafted free agent, I boarded a plane for Dallas to attend Spring Minicamp – the first step and obstacle in becoming a member of the fifty-three-man roster. I would soon be in the presence of several future Hall of Famers and Super Bowl Champions, a fact that didn't fully sink in until I had taken my seat on the plane. I remember staring out the airplane window beginning to understand the gravity of what I was walking into. My initial thoughts went to thanking God for opening the opportunity before me. On the heels of this, however, the doubts began creeping in, leading me to a darker place. I wasn't on this path alone. My family, hometown, and university were all walking alongside me, and while none of them (except my dad, ha) had any real expectations of success, I felt the pressure and anxiety of so many weighing heavy on my shoulders. Did I deserve this opportunity? Was I skilled enough? Big enough? Fast enough? Smart enough? Ready enough? After all, the famed "Valley Ranch," the Cowboys training facility, was a long way from my hometown of Snohomish, Washington.

REAL...REAL-ER...REAL-ER-ER!

I landed three and a half hours later in Dallas, TX expecting to hail a taxi to the rookie's hotel. Instead I was met by a driver holding up a Cowboys' sign in front of his chest. In a black dry-erase marker it read my name: Jeff Ogden. Sh*t just got real!

The following day I loaded onto one of the shuttle buses, bound for our training facility, that was crowded with grown men who *looked* the part of an NFL athlete. Men who, unlike myself, had to shave more than once a month… men whose bank account balances had several zeroes in them…men who had hardware on their fingers from college bowl victories and college championships, and possessed honors/awards from their respective universities. I, on the other hand, hadn't even needed to pack a razor and was wearing the same khaki shorts I had flown in the evening prior. Sh*t just got real-er!

I continued to look to God – and question whether or not He knew what He was doing – but I had to trust that He had a plan for me to be here. More importantly, I had prayed He wouldn't let me get my head knocked off. Any semblance of confidence I had left was quickly squashed as soon as I entered Valley Ranch's locker room. "Hey, can I get some new cleats?" I heard someone call in my direction. I glanced over at this returning veteran of the team and sheepishly corrected him. "I'm not an equipment guy, I'm a player." Sh*t just got real-er-er!

HUMILITY

DAY 1 AS A PROFESSIONAL FOOTBALL PLAYER

Typically, only rookies and a few veteran players who just joined the team attended Spring Minicamp practices, but with a new Head Coach and offensive system, the entire Cowboys' roster were also there that weekend. Over the course of the next three days which included five practices, we would wear only our helmets and shoulder pads, rather than the full football gear. The focus of the coaches was more on our skills than on seeing us hit one another. The goal for me and other rookies were to not get cut that weekend which would allow us a chance to attach ourselves to the fifty-three-man roster that fall.

MIND GAMES IN MINICAMP

My mentality and expectation going in to my first minicamp was that I would be "serviceable" for our defense and take repetitions for the starters while they took breathers. For all intents and purposes, I was a tackling dummy, and happy as hell to be just that. Any thoughts of actually making the team seemed a bit delusional. Later, I would liken it to when Rocky Balboa believed he was going to be Apollo Creed's sparring partner, only to learn he was going to get a shot at the title.

VIEW FROM THE STRETCHING LINES

Going into the first practice at Spring Minicamp I didn't have ANY expectation of being on the team after the final cuts in the fall. I was just looking forward to two things: putting a helmet with the lone star sticker on my head and running out of the tunnel at Texas Stadium. The latter almost didn't happen… details soon to come. Anyway, I was sitting with the other 100 players aspiring to be a Cowboy, stretching my quads, and just staring at that helmet, my hands itching to slip it on. I was so preoccupied with it, and the million other thoughts running through my mind, that I wasn't aware of what was happening around me, including the approach of Chan Gailey. The Head Coach was coming to acknowledge my existence by shaking my hand and introducing himself. Though he needed no introduction, I nearly failed to greet him because I was so enamored with the headgear lying on the ground next to my hip. My dream almost ended due to a daydream, ha.

One-On-NONE!

I was still feeling like this was all a dream as we began our first period of practice: One-On-One. This drill consisted of a quarterback, receiver, and a defender whose job was to stop me from catching the pass. It was man against man, or in my case, nervous boy against superheroes. As I stood in line, waiting for my route to be whispered to me by the quarterback, I bounced around to keep my muscles loose. Surrounding the drill on the sidelines of this closed-to-the public practice were several high-powered sponsors, executive personnel, and select individuals invited by the organization. Also present was Jerry Jones, the long-time owner of America's Team, who gazed onto the field in admiration of the new team he had assembled. But no pressure, right?!

It was about to happen: my first route as a professional football player. It was my first opportunity to live out my childhood dream, to make an impression on all the eyes that were focused on me. And an impression I did make!

Finally it was my turn, and I stepped up to get my route from the quarterback. In the first words he ever spoke to me, future Hall-of-Famer and three-time Super Bowl Champion Troy Aikman directed me with a slight Texan drawl, "Run a go route!" This meant I was to avoid the defender in front of me, run as fast as I could, and catch the ball forty to fifty yards down the field. Simple… or so I thought. As it turned out, that whole "avoid-the-defender" strategy is not that easy in the NFL.

STARING AT MY NEW OBSTACLE…DEION SANDERS

They say no man is an island, but the One-on-One drill may be an exception. As the name suggests, this practice pits man against man – each alone, an island unto himself. I keenly felt this isolation as I stood there, every muscle tensed, every ounce of focus on the defender crouched two feet in front of my chest. All eyes – and the camera operating from a crane on the sidelines – were upon us. There was nowhere to hide and the objective was crystal clear. Win. Beat the man in front of you. Catch the ball. If I catch the ball, I win. If I do not, the defender wins. Fistfights have arisen from this period of practice. Egos have been bruised and careers can be decided from that five-second meeting with destiny… In my case, the deliverer of that destiny is cornerback Deion Sanders, the best to ever play the position.

After receiving my directive, I trotted out to the line of scrimmage and focused my eyes and attention upon the QB who barked out his cadence. "Set, Hike!" The ball was snapped. Before I could begin to set my sights down the field or begin my "go route," I felt a jarring shock to my upper torso. The defender stopped me before I even moved. Laughs ensued on the sidelines, followed by high-fives by the other defenders waiting for their turns. I just stood there, not knowing what had just happened. As I gained my composure, I realized Deion Sanders was the obstacle in front of me. He had, without uttering a word, welcomed me to the NFL.

The coaches surrounding the drill let them have their laughs as they appointed a rookie defender to cover me next. I went back to the QB to get my directives. "Same thing," Aikman said, smirking. I immediately took my position. "Set, Hike!" I used my hands, feet, and adrenaline to overcome this new obstacle before me and, to my surprise, eluded the defender and began to distance myself in front of him. I was open – wide open! I began galloping up the sideline and noticed, out of the corner of my eye, all the sponsors, all the executives, some Cowboy Cheerleaders, and, of course, Jerry Jones. From there, everything played out in slow motion. I looked back to see Aikman's pass, the ball spiraling beautifully through the air as if he had full control over its trajectory. It gracefully reentered the earth's atmosphere and was due to land perfectly in my cradled arms… Reality soon set in again. The ball quickly fell directly through my arms and onto the field, where it bounced several times before settling fifteen to twenty yards away from me. Awkwardly, I began trying to corral this elusive ball like a farmer trying to catch a pig before making my way back to the receiver's line. Utterly humiliated, I imagined Jerry Jones' hand covering his face as he shook his head in disappointment. If emojis had existed back then, he might have inspired that often-used one of the palm covering the face.

When my turn came up again, a backup QB gave me a different route, a post route. Essentially, I was to run another deep route that aimed toward the goalpost in the opposite end zone. Another great pass sailed my way, only to meet the same fate. I dropped it. Again, I scampered to retrieve the ball from the turf then attempted to hide in the back of the receiver's line. When the first practice period of my professional football was about to end, I was assigned one last route-a simpler one. The QB called for a slant route, meaning my job was to run three steps, cut inside at a forty-five-degree angle and catch the ball. This route is a staple in every offense and one I had run a million times before. Simple…right? Nope! Another drop. With that drop the One-on-One practice period was over and, as I later learned, my career had almost ended prematurely as well. I only had myself to blame.

TIMEOUT - Overcoming Failure

"A surplus of effort could overcome a deficit of confidence."

~Sonia Sotomayor

I believe the "failures" in my life can, in hindsight, be viewed as mere challenges. If I counted every dropped ball; every mistake I've made as a father, brother or son; or my every insufficiency as a human, my life would permanently be defined as a failure. "Failing to be perfect" has allowed me to develop other strengths and mature mentally and spiritually. With this mindset I have learned to experience more joy in the victories and less pain in the defeats!

CHALK TALK

Did you know that ninety-nine percent of teams that have won the Super Bowl had losses during the regular season? Think about some "perceived failures" you have experienced in your life. Have you ever "dropped a ball?" Do you need to forgive yourself for anything? Forgive anyone else? Do you need to take ownership and accept where you're at right now? List them here. Next to them, write down what you did or can do to get back on your feet.

Ask for forgiveness, forgive yourself, learn from these defeats, and move on to the next challenge. What can you do to overcome feeling like a failure in the future?

_____

_____

_____

_____

_____

_____

_____

_____

_____

_____

_____

_____

_____

_____

_____

_____

_____

_____

_____

_____

_____

_____

_____

_____

VIEW FROM A ROOKIE HOTEL: EATING HUMBLE PIE

After a dismal performance at my first NFL practice, I returned to my hotel and tried to get a handle on the many thoughts and emotions racing through my head. I was angry at myself and even angrier at God, who I felt had let me down. "I have conditioned every day," I said, eyes to the ceiling, "I have eaten as clean as I could. I avoided late nights with friends. I have dedicated myself to learning not only my position, but others as well. I have worked too hard to be embarrassed!" The words had no sooner left my lips when I realized that everything I'd said in my little rant was about me. "I did this… I did that." In actuality, what I had really done was take my eyes off the prize. God reminded me that it was by His strength that I was in this unique position. It was by His strength that I was to fulfill His plans, whatever they may be for me. Yes, I'd been humbled that day on the field, but not nearly as humbled as I was while laying in bed at the rookies' hotel.

COWBOYS SPRING MINICAMP, DAY 2

The following day I approached practice from a position of humility. My objective now was not to seek out my selfish goals, but to fulfill the plan of a God who had my best interest in mind.

Again, our first practice period was One-on-One. I received a five-yard hitch route from the quarterback: which meant sprint five yards, stop, look for, and catch the ball. I completed the route and looked for the football, only it was nowhere near me. Then, in what I can only compare to a scene from the Matrix, I levitated horizontally to the turf, stretched out my arms behind me, and somehow found the ball stuck in my hands. Amazed and slightly stunned by what had just happened, I jogged back to hand the ball to the quarterback, received a slap on the butt, and took my place in the back of the receiver's line. Amidst the cheers and looks of approval from the players and spectators, I smiled and thanked God. No, I could not do this by my strength alone, and He had just confirmed how in control He was.

I had a multi-faceted belief system that provided me strength, confidence, and requisite skills needed to give me the best chance of being successful. I had my faith, my work ethic, and talents. I know not everyone reading this will share the same belief system. However, I urge all readers to find their higher power, draw from positive teachings, and use them to maximize your talents – be it professionally, academically, or personally.

I'm unable to recall many other details from that spring minicamp. I was told, however, that there was serious discussion amongst the coaches as to whether or not I would be cut that weekend. It wasn't uncommon for that to happen, and it did happen to a few other players after that minicamp. As it turned out, I was barely good enough to act as a "tackling dummy." Ouch.

Up to this point, I had overcome health obstacles I had as a child. I had overcome several obstacles that nearly derailed me from playing college football. I had overcome the obstacle of dropped passes in spring minicamp. The stage was now set for me to face my biggest football obstacle: the official 1998 Dallas Cowboys Fall Training Camp. There, I would be tested like never before.

MINDGAMES: "THE MORE YOU CAN DO"

"The more you can do" is a common phrase used in the NFL. A team was only allowed to suit up forty-five of the fifty-three players on the roster for each game. (Note: That number has since changed.) That means if you are wearing a uniform on Sunday, you will be playing on offense, defense, special teams, or a combination of the three. For me, an undrafted rookie, I knew my value to the team would be in learning several different offensive positions as well as contributing on as many special teams as possible...*the more I can do!* The "special teams" consist of the kicking games, including kickoffs, punts, and field goals. Not having played on any special teams in college, this would be a huge challenge for me. In the Cowboys' new offense, I made a point to learn each receiver's responsibilities as well as the running back's position. On special teams I began my acquisition of punt- and kick-catching skills, as well as covering kicks and punts (tackling kick and punt returners). I had a very short window to show the Cowboys that I could contribute on a level that met the expectations of a Super Bowl-caliber team. "The more you can do" has forever been embedded in my brain and continue to use it off the field as well.

MIND GAMES... HEADING INTO THE PRESEASON

In the NFL there were five pre-season games leading up to a regular season campaign. The outcomes of these games were inconsequential. For me, a first-year rookie, the goal during the pre-season was to not get cut and keep my dream alive for another week. I placed my focus on proving to the coaches that I belonged and could contribute to the team. I had to find any way to get out on the field, be it offense or special teams. This mindset can be a catch-22 (pun *intended*). On one hand, getting on the field would give me the best opportunity to make plays and stay relevant to those who make the decisions on the fifty-three-man roster. On the other hand, there was a very real possibility that I would demonstrate a *lack* of requisite skill to make it in the NFL. If I was to make a team as an undrafted player, I chose to take fate into one of my hands... while grasping God's with the other.

FALL TRAINING CAMP (July 1998)

"Life doesn't get easier or more forgiving; we get stronger and more resilient."

~Dr. Steve Maraboli

Day one of training camp was comprised mostly of logistics, with players checking in and getting dorm assignments, a brief orientation, and weekly practice schedules. Rookies usually arrived in modest vehicles, with just a few suitcases and bags. As I did not own a car, I hitched a ride with another player, and just as I had at the spring minicamp, arrived with a small carry-on duffle bag. Some of the "superstars" made a more dramatic entrance. One such player stepped right from a stretch limousine and onto his customized Mercedes golf cart, speakers blaring. Another felt that taking to the air was a more convenient way to travel and arrived via helicopter.

I was catching a glimpse of what life could be like for those in the NFL. Now, if only I could catch the footballs.

IT'S GETTING HOT IN HERE

In the summer of 1998, Wichita Falls, Texas was in the midst of a record heatwave, with the temperature topping a hundred degrees for thirty-one straight days. Unfortunately, training camp coincided directly with this historic heat. In anticipation of this unexpected challenge, players were required to weigh in before and after each practice to ensure proper hydration had been achieved. The first morning practice was scheduled as a "full gear" practice, which in the NFL meant we had to wear helmets, shoulder pads, and our football pants, just as we would in a game. What a relief, I thought, that we wouldn't have to wear the butt pad, hip pads, thigh, and kneepads required during my college days. Yet despite the elimination of this protective gear, the heat would prove to be too much for me on Day 1.

Following a two-and-a-half-hour practice that required me to perform at a high level on offense and special teams, I weighed in eight pounds shy of my pre-practice weight. I was then given IVs of saline solution in both arms. Later, I will discuss, in too much detail, the only other time that happened to me – a game where I didn't make it out to the field in time to receive the second-half kickoff.

MEMORIZING THE PHONEBOOK... I MEAN "PLAYBOOK"

During training camp, unless I was on the field, I carried my playbook everywhere – to the training room, while getting my ankles taped or rehabbing an injury, the cafeteria, the dormitory, on the bus – everywhere. It should be noted that these playbooks are the size of phonebooks, their pages printed front and back with terminology, philosophy, and plays in different formations and alignments. Each play has many variations and responsibilities that differ depending on the defensive schemes. These alterations in the plays can happen pre-snap (before the ball is hiked) *and* afterward the ball is hiked. I cannot describe the difficulties that defenses present once the play has begun. Not only did I have to memorize each play, but also the play I would have to pivot to in the fraction of a second if the defense disguised their strategy.

During the regular season, practices occurred once per day for two and a half hours. However, there is little to no downtime. Instead, we would spend every minute of the ten-hour day receiving physical therapy, or in meetings watching opponent film, and studying new gameplans. Each week, we would receive a new, specific "phonebook" containing plays that would give us the best chance to defeat our next opponent the following Sunday.

FALL TRAINING CAMP, DAY 2

"When you say 'YES' to others, make sure you are not saying 'NO' to yourself."

~Paulo Coelho

They say people tend to want what they can't have, and I am no exception. A quadriceps injury that occurred on day two had ended my participation for the next ten practice sessions. Injuries are a player's greatest fear – well, aside from The Turk (more on him later) – and this one was devastating to me. I saw my role as having two main components: act as tackling dummy for the defense and give breaks to the starters. I was of no value to the Cowboys sitting on the sidelines and training table. I felt I was being labeled as weak, "soft," and unable to tolerate pain. Making matters worse was the fact that my fellow wide receivers had to pick up my slack in the hundred-degree heat. A majority of the time when an undrafted free agent sustains any type of injury, the team will release that player, offer him a small settlement check, and bring in another 'tackling dummy' to take his place. Fortunately, I was granted the opportunity to rehab my quad and encouraged to heal – *very* quickly! – by my coaches. Our amazing training and rehabilitation staff worked on me day and night with few breaks in between. I returned to the practice field eight days later. Although I battled nagging muscle injuries in both hamstrings throughout the rest of training camp, I was fortunate enough to not miss any more practice time.

It was now time to compete with the other ninety-five football players vying for employment with the 1998 Dallas Cowboys.

SCOUTING YOUR EVERY MOVE

I'm uncertain if this holds true for every organization, but the Cowboys employed scouts to evaluate each player during every practice at training camp. These scouts, who had already tested the rookies at their respective colleges, would now stand behind the offensive huddle with clipboard and pen in hand, discussing how they looked physically (did they pass the "eye test?"); carried themselves and responded to being coached; how much they hustled and how they related to teammates; et cetera. Every catch was recorded, as well as every drop. Not only did they count the yards of the catch, but also the Yards *After* the Catch (YAC). Every detail, including mental mistakes and missed blocks, was summarized at the end of each practice; we would then be given our statistics during the evening meeting. Needless to say, being under this type of scrutiny was stressful; it was also excellent preparation for life in the NFL. I dealt with it by treating each practice as if it were an actual game. I went full speed with every opportunity, knowing this was my best chance at getting noticed.

THE SEASON BEFORE THE SEASON

The typical football season at Eastern Washington University had consisted of ten games. That fall, I played in seven "games" (five preseason games and two scrimmages) with the Cowboys before the 1998 regular season even started. This allowed me ample opportunities to demonstrate my abilities, but it could also expose my weaknesses. The demands of training camp challenged me mentally and physically in a way I had never imagined. Here's what a typical day at training camp looked like:

5:30a Wake-up call

6:00a Treatment & rehab

7:00a Breakfast

7:30a Offensive Installment Meeting (reviewing new plays for both practices)

8:30a Treatment, rehab, get ankles taped for practice (while studying new plays)

9:30a Morning practice

Noon Ice bath, treatment & rehab

12:50p "To-go" Lunch (I ate it in my room while studying)

1:30p Film review of morning practice

3:00p Treatment & rehab; study new plays, get ankles taped

4:00p Evening practice

6:00p Ice bath, treatment & rehab

7:00p Dinner

7:30p Special Teams Meeting

8:00p Film review of evening practice

10:00p Treatment & rehab

11:00p Study playbook

Midnight: Lights out

Each day felt like a week. For me, an undrafted rookie, there was no rest... no time to relax... no time to waste... no margin of error... no distractions. Proving myself worthy of the Cowboys' fifty-three-man roster felt like an insurmountable obstacle, and I felt every bit of it mentally, physically and, eventually, emotionally.

WRONG SIDE OF A CUSS-OUT

It's easy to look back and laugh at it now, but at the time I nearly cried. During one of our practices at training camp, our Special Team's coach had called for the Punt Return team to take the field. (I had been solely focused on the art of catching punts that I failed to properly learn every other position on the punt return team. (Remember the mantra: "The more you can do!") I lined up as a punt-blocker on the end of the line of scrimmage. Coach called for a particular punt block, and I looked to the player next to me to make sure I was lined up properly. I was, but the coach overheard my uncertainty and decided to make an example out of me. There, in front of five thousand fans, he proceeded to chew my butt into the ground, with a resounding roar and use of every expletive in the English language. His outbursts were legendary and the crowd was entertained, but I had never been so embarrassed or humiliated in my entire life.

TIMEOUT

Michael Jordan scored only two points, making one out of nine of his shots during the worst game of his career. At the Masters golf tournament Tiger Woods scored a ten on a par-3. He finished fifty-seventh overall. Tom Brady threw three interceptions and no touchdowns in a 38-3 loss to the Saints in 2020 – the worst loss in both his college or NFL careers. I was humiliated that afternoon after being cussed out and I had to make a choice right then and there how I would handle it.

CHALK TALK

We all know that the Tampa Bay Buccaneers, led by Tom Brady, went on to win the Super Bowl, where he earned MVP honors. Michael Jordan and Tiger Woods have made history with their illustrious careers. Bouncing back from bad games, missed shots, dropped balls, and even cuss-outs is a sign of a mentally strong individual. How have you handled ridicule in the past? What actions might you take when your performance at work, in relationships, or on the field suffers? I chose to take my cuss-out as a challenge, and the coaches noticed my mental toughness.

1ST PRESEASON GAME

TUNNEL VISION

I had now made it through the first few weeks of training camp. I had survived the physical pain, mental strains, and emotional hardships doled out by my special teams coach and, somehow, made it to my very first game day- a pre-season matchup against my hometown team, the Seattle Seahawks.

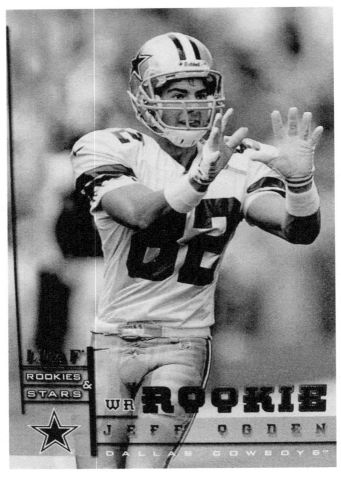

Please let me catch this!

This was no ordinary preseason game for me, but was a culmination of, and a salute to, every obstacle that once lay before me. In my estimation, my days of playing football would be done after this game. I would be given my walking papers when first cuts happened the following day. But at that moment I didn't care, because within a matter of hours a life-long dream would finally come true. A dream I was fortunate enough to live out, not only for myself, but for my family, college, hometown, and every other average boy who cradled a football. I would get to buckle my chinstrap that secured the sacred starred helmet to my head. I would trot down the tunnel at Texas Stadium with a multitude of future Hall-of-Famers. I would seemingly float out into the sold-out stadium. I would run through a lineup of the most beautiful women I had ever seen, the world-famous Dallas Cowboy Cheerleaders. I would be on national TV playing against my hometown and favorite team, the Seattle Seahawks. No pressure...yeah, right. Sh*t just got real-est!

Banner that hung at first preseason game of my rookie year, 1998.

"THEY BOTH MESSED UP, BUT WERE ON THE SAME PAGE."

My first – and what I thought would be my last – game, couldn't have played out any better. As I stood on the sideline before the game, I glanced up into the endzone, just taking in the moment, and that's when I saw a four-by-eight-foot banner draped over the lower level that read, "Official Fan Club of Jeff Ogden." Two of my fellow rookies were included on the banner as well. This both humbled me and made me feel like I was walking on air; it made the moment even more surreal.

It was during the second half of the game that I would see my first action. Any muscle pain or joint ailment vanished as I took to the field for the first time. I remember thinking that the Seahawks' defense looked huge! Remembering my mom's advice, my intention was to run and avoid them as much as humanly possible.

"RUN JEFFY, RUN!"

Growing up, my mom wasn't all that thrilled with the prospect of me playing football – she was terrified that her "baby" would get injured. In her eyes, I was still the undersized asthmatic and sickly kid who could barely walk properly. Plus she had already been witness to my brother breaking his arm playing high school football and didn't want to see me follow in his footsteps. It may sound funny, but the advice she issued before my first preseason game against the Seattle Seahawks stuck with me throughout my NFL career: "Jeffy, when those big boys are chasing you, you just run away!" I did, and fortunately I did it pretty well.

My first catch came very soon after entering the game. It was a simple hitch route. My job was to run five yards, stop, and catch it. My quarterback, who was also my roommate during training camp, chose to throw it in my direction. It was his first passing attempt and completion and my first catch in the NFL. After catching the ball, I scampered around, avoiding the big boys inside, and had a nice gain. Later in the game, we were driving deep into Seahawks territory close to their goal line. We rookies hadn't had extensive practice in operating the 'red-zone offense' (an offensive scheme used when inside the opponent's twenty-yard line.) Our QB called a play. I lined up at a position I hadn't practiced much, then the ball was snapped. Confused, I entered the zone where I'd vowed I would never go. I ran directly into the middle of Big Boy Land. After scrambling around, our QB threw the ball through three defenders and it found its way into my outstretched arms. I fell forward and found myself just inches from scoring a touchdown. The next play called for our running back to bully his way into the end zone for a touchdown, and he did just that.

"When those big boys are chasing you, just run away!"
Best advice from my mom.

I have no idea what the score of the game ended up being, but my first game as a professional NFL football player was over. I had finished it with a few catches, no drops, and a couple of good Special Teams plays. Again, I saw the Fan Club banner hanging in the endzone as I walked back toward the tunnel. I couldn't stop smiling.

After the game, our Head Coach was asked about how he thought his young players played that night – me and my QB roommate in particular. Careful not to praise us too much, he replied (and I am paraphrasing here), "The ball was thrown and caught, but they both made mental mistakes on that play down there in the red zone…they messed up, but at least they were on the same page."

INSTANT REPLAY- JERRY'S WORLD

Inevitably, cut-down days always come. Traditionally, this pairing-down process comes in a series of three waves. The first wave is the biggest, with around twenty players being sent home. The second wave sees that number drop to around sixty, then the final cut leaves fifty-three men who will comprise that year's squad. Leading up to the first round of cuts, I embarrassed myself once again. It seems that my naive nature and sheltered life led me into situations that I wish I could redo. During one of our training camp practices, Jerry Jones, the owner of the Cowboys, rode his golf cart along the sideline. He looked my way and said with a smirk, "Don't you go on and make this team now, Jeff!" Caught off guard, I responded, "Yes sir, I won't!" Bahahaha… *dammit!*

END OF PRESEASON

THE TURK

Before we move on, there is an individual who is universally despised around the NFL. A man who determines, without debate, the immediate future of every single player with whom he comes into contact. His job description, as it relates to this role, is not a desirable one. His name is rarely spoken aloud, as if it might summon him like some fabled monster. This individual, whom every man avoided at all costs, was known as "The Turk." At the Valley Ranch practice facility, the players entered through one door. On cut day, The Turk would stand just inside those doors holding a sheet of paper. If your name was called out as you walked in, you were directed to grab your playbook and go see Coach. This meant one thing: you had been cut, and your services were no longer needed by the Dallas Cowboys. It was during these entrances that careers were ended, friendships diverged, and hearts were broken. Surely this man loathed his role, but not nearly as much as we loathed that sinking feeling, wondering if the next name he called would be our own.

Up to this point, after four preseason games, my name had managed to elude The Turk's mouth. I can't recall many details from the three preseason games following the Seahawks, but obviously I'd performed well enough to pass muster. Each game had been increasingly important, but this next one felt different. It *was* different. The only things now standing between me making the Cowboy's fifty-three-man roster was the Jacksonville Jaguars and a few veteran receivers whose fate would also be determined in the days following the game.

PUT ME IN, COACH, I'M READY TO PLAY!

For the final game of the preseason, the plan was for the veterans to play the first half, then I would get most of the plays in the second half. However, it would "play out" quite differently. After some poor plays and dropped footballs in the first half, I was feeling even antsier to get out on the field. While standing, as I usually did, next to my receiver's coach, he yelled out for a receiver to enter the game. Apparently, we broke the huddle with only ten players on the field; the eleventh, the missing receiver, was receiving treatment for an injury on the bench.

Seeing my opportunity, I said, "I got it!" Little did I know at the time that I was entering the game at a position I didn't normally play. Our

QB whispered the play in my ear as I ran out to take my position. It was a "simple" hitch route. At this point, the Jaguars still had a majority of their starters in the game. I surveyed the defense, pretending I knew what I was doing (Ha) and trying to look the part of an NFL wide receiver. My defender was lined up directly in front of me about eight yards away. I knew my job was to sprint five yards, stop, turn, and expect the pass to come my way. The quarterback's job was to pick a side, then throw the ball to the receiver who had the best chance of being open. Since I was on the side closest to the QB, I liked my chances of getting the ball thrown my way. The noise of the crowd, the defense yelling out their adjustments, and the orders from the coaches on the sidelines dissipated. That's when the edges of my eyes blurred and reality played out in slow motion.

"NEXT MAN UP!"

"Next Man Up" is a widely-used phrase that teams use to motivate and encourage their backup players. In many sports, particularly football, injuries happen. Mistakes happen. When these things occur, the next man up is expected to be prepared and fill in without weakening the team. In my final preseason game, I was that guy, the Next Man Up. One accomplished veteran had dropped a wide-open pass that would've ended with him trotting into the endzone. Following that unfortunate mistake, another receiver was hit by a defender after dropping a pass and had to leave the game. He never returned. All the studying, all the pushing through the pain and the grueling one hundred-degree, two-a-day practices, along with my "the more you can do" mentality, had prepared me for this moment.

I knew my responsibility and my route. What I didn't account for was the "adjustments" that the hitch route had assigned to it. If the defender backed up at the snap of the ball, I would stop at five yards. If he didn't, I would have to make an adjustment to my route. In this case, the defender never moved; he just sat at his depth of eight yards and waited for me in a crouched stance. He disguised his intentions until after the ball was hiked/snapped. Recognizing his technique, I knew my route needed to be adjusted. No longer was I to run five yards and stop; now I had to run as fast as I could, evade the defender, and expect to catch the ball forty to fifty yards down the field. (The same route that I ran in my first minicamp where I dropped the pass.) Suddenly, as the ball was hiked back to the QB, everything began to unfold in slow motion, just as it had during my very first repetition at spring minicamp, but this time Jerry Jones wasn't on the sidelines – neither were the sponsors or cheerleaders. It was just me and my defender, both breathing heavily and hand fighting while jockeying for position as we sprinted down the field. I had him in my right back pocket, meaning that I was ahead of him by about one foot but still close enough that he could feel me.

To my surprise, as I turned to look back toward the quarterback, I saw the ball hanging in the air, spiraling down toward me. Only problem was, my defender saw the same thing and he planned on doing anything he could to prevent me from catching it. The ball neared and I felt his hands reach and grasp onto my right arm. Falling to the ground, I extended my left arm out toward the ball. In a fraction of a second, my hours of hard work, training, and dedication paid off. I was able to corral the ball in with one arm as we both slammed onto the turf. That catch accounted for a large part of my sixty-one yards that day, which led all the receivers. Later, I would learn that our Head Coach radioed down from the press box to the other coaches on the field, "Oggie just made the team with that catch!" My first attempt running that route had nearly gotten me fired during spring minicamp before my career had begun – now the same route secured a dream, a job, and changed the trajectory of my life.

FINAL CUTS

After our last preseason game versus the Jacksonville Jaguars on Saturday night, the final cuts loomed over my head. A training camp that began with around one hundred players would soon be reduced to the final fifty-three-man roster on Monday morning. Needless to say, I didn't get much sleep that weekend.

Monday arrived. The few left in the rookie hotel boarded the passenger van knowing that The Turk would be standing in the entryway of the practice facility, clipboard in hand, waiting to pick players off as they walked in. Everything hinged on that ten-yard walk from the van to the glass double doors. Spring minicamp, fall training camp, scrimmages, and preseason games would all factor into the coaches' decisions of who would remain a Dallas Cowboy.

I couldn't feel my legs as I walked toward the glass doors to the facility that day; however, I could feel my heart beating out of my chest. I pulled open the door, which somehow felt heavier than normal, to see The Turk standing there. As I approached, he called out in an ominous voice that in my mind was in slow motion, J o h n n y... G o S e e C o a c h. ???

Wait, my name's not Johnny. Did he not see me? Did he not know who I was or know my name?

Not wanting to stick around for what I felt was inevitable, I quickly scampered by him and sat at my locker where I attempted to hide behind my practice jersey hanging on a hook. As I looked around the locker room, I noticed several things. First, there were a lot of empty lockers. The nameplate of my locker buddy, a fellow rookie wide receiver, had been removed from our locker. Mine remained. I also noticed that most of the guys were acting as if it was just another normal day. I, on the other hand, felt completely out of place. Not knowing what to do next, I put on my practice uniform and took several deep breaths. After what seemed to be the longest twenty minutes of my life, I began walking to our morning team meeting. On the way, I noticed that everyone was in street clothes. Dang it. I rushed back to my locker, took off my uniform, threw on a Cowboys T-shirt and headed back to the meeting room. I remember sitting crouched low in my seat. I looked around and saw future Hall- of-Famers Michael Irvin, Troy Aikman, Emmitt Smith, Larry Allen, Deion Sanders, and many other Super Bowl champions. Was this really happening? There I was, a presumed tackling dummy from the small town of Snohomish, Washington sitting amongst several all-time great players. Was I actually going to see my dream fulfilled? My heart was still beating out of my chest.

It all sunk in when I caught Coach Gailey's eye and he didn't immediately kick me out of the room. Instead, he said, "Gentleman, welcome to the 1998 Dallas Cowboys!"

"JEFF, IT'S GOD... NO ONE'S HOME!"

It was all I could do to hold back my emotions as we took to the field for a light practice after that meeting. A short two hours later, I, along with one other rookie, rode the van back to the rookie hotel. I barely made it to my room before I broke down. I fell onto my freshly made, queen-sized bed and bawled. I could not believe this had happened. I was a Dallas Cowboy. I got to wear a star on my helmet. I immediately picked up the hotel phone to call my parents. It was midday on a Monday, so no one answered our home phone. Next, I tried my brother...no luck. My agent?.. Nope! I exhausted my list of people to call. As I laid back onto the pillows of my bed, a realization hit me. I felt God was vying for my attention. He wanted my priority to remain in Him and *His* ultimate plan. This plan didn't end with me playing professional football. The NFL was just a vehicle I would ride in order to influence and change people's lives in a positive way... It was God's car, so I called "shotgun!"

TIMEOUT - Overcoming Setbacks by Maximizing Potential

I have had opponents who provided obstacles; however, I've been able to overcome their resistance by putting in the work to improve my craft – developing my skills; training smarter, longer and harder, and studying game plans. I compete against my potential. If I do not maximize my potential, it is only then that I lose. All too often, there is the smallest difference between success and perceived failures.

212 DEGREES

At 211 degrees, water is just water. Add one degree and that water becomes steam which can power a locomotive!

CHALK TALK

Are you maximizing your time? How might you be able to be more efficient? What's your 212th degree" that could provide you an edge? Block out time and prioritize yourself. It's not you versus the world... it's you versus that moment.

HALFTIME

This section is a compilation of "odds and ends" stories from my life in the NFL. There is no rhyme or reason to their order – I just think they're interesting, funny, and oftentimes humiliating, and I offer them up for your enjoyment.

BBOC – "BEST BUNS ON CAMPUS"

It was right before my second year with the Cowboys, and the team was at Training Camp on the campus of Midwestern State University. We had just broken the team huddle following the morning practice when we were greeted by a Cowboy's marketing director, along with several cameras and reporters. This wouldn't have been at all unusual if they were looking for Troy Aikman or Emmitt Smith, but they weren't. They were looking for *me*. My surprise turned to confusion when they presented me with a t-shirt that read "1999 BBOC." Apparently, fans, along with some media outlets, had voted me as having the Best Buns on Campus. They then asked me how I felt about being recognized for these "attributes." Though completely caught off guard, I'd like to think I offered a smooth answer: "I'd first like to thank our Strength and Conditioning Coach, who made me perform a million squats and lunges throughout the off-season. My mom would be so proud of me if she could be here now!" Though I thought it was silly to be recognized for this award, my self-esteem got a huge boost, ha.

OF COURSE I PAINT MY TOENAILS

Following each season in the NFL, I contemplated retirement. Unlike collegiate football, when I played purely for the love of the game, it was now my job, my business. I was the CEO of my own corporation, and every decision, every action, and every play on the field would determine my company's success. As its sole employee, everything fell on my shoulders, including the expectations of family, friends, teammates, organizations, and fans, all of whom were heavily invested in my success. Under the weight of this great responsibility and pressure, football had ceased to be "just a game."

Peytan Starr in her cheerleaders dress in Baltimore.

Following my third year in the NFL I didn't feel as though my job was at risk (something really bad would have had to happen for me to not secure a roster spot on the 2001 Dolphins roster.) Now, my only "business" goal, and deepest desire, was to become a "vested" player. To do this, one must play for three years plus an additional six games into their fourth, thus unlocking a treasure trove of future benefits, including a pension, medical benefits, annuities, and so on. Obviously, this is an extremely important milestone, and at this point I had only six more games before I reached it. Indeed, there was much on the line as I worked to support "Jeff Ogden, Inc.," and it was precisely then that my body decided to revolt against the stress and strain my chosen occupation had placed on it.

On October 28, 2001, I became a vested player in the NFL! Ironically, it came against my hometown team, the Seattle Seahawks, who we bested with a 24-20 victory. But I still left smiling with two huge ice bags on my knees.

During my fourth training camp, my mind and body began faltering. The two-a-day practices in the South Florida heat had become increasingly taxing. My knees had trouble running routes. My shoulder's range of motion was severely limited. My brain was fried from the constant stress and anxiety. Realizing that I needed some way to motivate myself, I did what any NFL player would do. I painted my big toes bright red!

This bold, brave, and nonsensical idea served two purposes. One, it helped strengthen the toenails themselves (I would lose my big toenails during each fall training camp due to the constant impact and pressure on them), and two, it would remind me why I had chosen to play another season and put myself through this agonizing journey.

Each day, twice a day, I and the other players would head to the training room to get our ankles taped to help prevent sprains. Every time I hopped up on that table, the red nail polish would remind me why I was playing another season. I took that time to pray. I'd ask God to give me strength, energy, and mental focus. I wanted to provide for my daughter.

Doors would remain open as long as I had my platform as an NFL athlete. Schools would still want me to deliver motivational speeches. Churches would still invite me to give my testimony. My foundation would continue to receive funds that helped place foster children into permanent homes. A lot was at stake, yes, but none of it was about *me*. It was in God's hands. Who would have thought He would use those hands to paint my toenails bright red?

MIAMI DOLPHINS FIGHT SONG

Okay, by now you've probably realized that I'm a bit peculiar. This story will further validate that belief. Having been diagnosed with ADHD, I can find football games a bit overstimulating. Whether I was on the field or on the sideline, I noticed, and was distracted by, everything around me. For some reason, I became mesmerized by the Dolphin's fight song that was played after touchdowns, so much so that after a score you would've seen me mouthing the words: "…And when you say Miami you're talking Super Bowl… Miami Dolphins number one!" After my punt-return touchdown in 2000, I was out of breath…I was receiving hugs, slaps on the butt and helmet…and could hear the roar of the seventy-three thousand fans. Yet, as excited and grateful as I was for it all, I just wanted to hear one thing: The Dolphins Fight Song. After placing an oxygen mask on my face, I sat on the bench and lost myself in that beautiful music. There was only one audio clip that would eclipse the pleasure I experienced at that moment, and it came the same night on ESPN.

I…COULD…GO…All…THE…WAY?

When thinking about ESPN, the worldwide leader in sports television, there is one name that stands out amongst broadcasters. Chris Berman, aka The G.O.A.T, had a way of reviewing the highlights of games unlike any other. He coined hundreds of names and phrases that are staples in the sports world. Having Chris Berman describe a play on ESPN was like

Frank Sinatra performing at your wedding… at least to me, ha. One of his most well-known phrases came when a player would score a touchdown running a long way to the end zone: "He could go…all…the…way," said with deliberate long pauses. I had the amazing pleasure of hearing him describe my punt return in that manner. As silly as it may sound, it was a dream come true to experience that. I have no doubt he's reading this, so thank you, Mr. Berman ;)

NAKED AT A GAME

The only distraction we had from the cold that day was the Bills fans, who, thanks to the help of some "warming-fluid" served at the concession stands, did not seem to be affected by the extreme temperatures. They certainly had plenty of energy to hurl eggs and snowballs at our team bus as we arrived at the stadium! Then, in the third quarter of our game, we all heard a bunch of cheering and clapping – which was odd as the game had been paused for a commercial break so there was no action on the field. We looked into the stands and there, about fifteen rows up, we found the cause of the applause. In the snowy, near zero-degree temperature, a woman decided she was bored… or maybe she was just hot, because she'd felt it necessary to remove all clothing from the waist up. After the cheers, laughter, and clapping subsided she was instructed by the security team (and I'm sure her husband) to cover back up. Surprisingly, she wasn't escorted out, but I'm sure the concession stands were off-limits to her for the rest of the game

STEROIDS & THE BEST MOVE IN FOOTBALL

I have never been accused of taking steroids, for obvious reasons, ha. However, I have been asked more than once how many NFL players take them. The best answer I had came from a coach: "The best move in football is SPEED!" A wide receiver can have the most amazing hands in the world. He could catch a ball with one hand, no hands, in between his legs, in his facemask, behind his back, no matter what. But if he can't beat his defender and get open, he'll never have that opportunity. Speed can make a poorly run route look much better. A receiver can complement his good pass-catching hands with great speed and play a long time in the NFL.

A kick returner can catch a kick and read the blocking perfectly, but if he's not fast enough to run through the holes, he will get his head knocked off. Speed can prevent injuries from hits, and ensure the kick returner keeps his job. The term "Speed Kills" is never overstated in the NFL.

Players at the NFL level are freaks of nature. I looked at them in awe. The sheer space they occupy...the strength they possess...and the speed at which they move, is unlike anything I've ever seen. They are ridiculously skilled and talented, and the physical attributes are what separates them from the rest of the "normal" population.

All of that being said, to my knowledge, I've never known of any player using steroids. In my opinion, it is not on any list of necessities to play in the NFL. Muscles need to be long and flexible. They need to contract quickly and powerfully. They need to survive hundreds of explosive repetitions per day for six months every year of a player's career.

Aside from all the negative side-effects, it would be nearly impossible to fool the NFL. The team knew where I was at all times, even in the off-season. If I was on vacation in Hawaii, the NFL could have me scheduled to submit a urine sample on that same day. I would then be required to allow an independent and approved doctor to come to my location. There, he would literally watch the urine exit my body and into a sample bottle. After being sealed, it would then be tested for any performance-enhancing drugs and "recreational" ones as well. Our team staff was very diligent in addressing banned substances, as it wasn't just steroids or illegal drugs that could cause suspensions and fines. There are certain over-the-counter medicines, and even foods, that can trigger a red flag in a urine sample. To be safe, players would be instructed to only use supplements that were issued by team doctors and trainers.

To this day, I have never seen steroids or have knowledge of anyone ever using them. They don't make sense, and they're definitely not worth it.

TIMEOUT: CRUTCHES

"Self-care is not selfish. You cannot serve from an empty vessel."

-Eleanor Brownn

In this book I've talked about how I overcame obstacles that were placed in my path; sometimes, however, the pressures of life caused me to create my own obstacles. As a professional athlete, I had to handle the fame, fans, social life, and so on, all while performing at the highest level on the field, and in response I developed "coping mechanisms" that were not always in my best interest and actually blocked my growth. To combat these, I had to first recognize what I was doing, then formulate a plan to eradicate my poor choices. Outlets such as unhealthy behaviors and substance abuse provide temporary relief but may cause permanent damage. Life will present us with more than enough obstacles; we don't need to create any more of them!

CHALK TALK

Take inventory of your obstacles. Are there any that are self-made? Are there any that you can eliminate on your own? Are there any that may require assistance from a loved one, therapist, or program? List these obstacles along with a plan to remove them, and a specific date they will be accomplished.

_____

_____

_____

_____

_____

_____

PRE-GAME MEALS

One of the most enjoyable aspects of my career was the team meals leading up to a game. We had two mandatory team meals: dinner on Saturdays and breakfast on Sundays. Keep in mind that we didn't monitor intake, calculate calories, or made sure we ate all our veggies… or at least I didn't. I was a young, single man who didn't really know how to cook – most evenings I ate French toast and eggs – so meals with some variety, and endless proportions, were a much-anticipated treat. After writing out the following meals, I can say that, perhaps, I over-indulged a bit! Below is a typical dinner and pre-game breakfast:

Saturday Evening Dinner

Burger with two slices of cheese and fries

Two chicken drumsticks

Two slices of pepperoni and veggie pizza (see, I did get some veggies!)

Fruit (strawberries, blackberries, grapes)

Brownie with vanilla ice cream

Cookies and two small cartons of milk (snack before bed)

Pre-game Breakfast

Omelet Bar (bacon, cheese, mushrooms, olives)

Hash browns

French toast with berries

Side of bacon (I needed more than what they put in the omelet, ha)

Yogurt

Thankfully, my metabolism was pretty high back then… and so was my cholesterol and blood pressure! Ha. Looking back, I could eat quite a bit, but compared to the big boys, I was just nibbling.

BLUE FOOTBALL FIELD

Boise State University is home to a very unique field. It is a bright blue turf – so blue that many birds have mistaken it for a body of water and dove to their death. (This has caused many to protest for obvious reasons.) Boise State was a division above my college football team, so traveling there to play in front of much bigger crowds and on that unique turf would be unforgettable. That wasn't the case for me. Recently, I was reminiscing with my college quarterback, and I said I wished I had played on the blue turf at Boise State. His response: "You did, idiot." – or something to that effect. I remained adamant, and even wagered my home on it. While on the phone, he texted over a picture that showed us together on the blue turf. I learned that day not to make any wagers – luckily, I was able to keep my home as I did not give him my address.

FLIRTY COLLEGE KID

I did have some unique training methods, one of which I shared during a TV interview in Dallas. When they asked me how I had developed such "good hands," I told them how, during my junior year of college, I found out that I had a fifth stress fracture in my lower back. I was forced to sit out that season while the vertebrae healed itself, and I was also limited to certain exercises.

While doing some conditioning in our indoor fieldhouse, I noticed a pretty tennis player. She too was injured, and limited to just serving tennis balls over the net. My idea of flirting was to show off, apparently. I stood on the opposite side of the net and asked her if I could catch the balls and throw them back to her. After all, she had a brace on her knee, so I was just being a gentleman, right? She humored me and began hitting the balls over with extreme velocity. My attempt at being a macho football player failed miserably. I could barely see the balls, let alone catch them. My eye-hand coordination improved over time, and unfortunately, so did my rehab crush's knee. After a couple weeks, I had gained a new skill, but lost a chance for a date off the tennis courts, ha.

All kidding aside, I looked for any opportunity to improve at the game I loved. I wanted to be better. I *had* to be better if I expected a chance to play. During the off-season in college, we had a brutal conditioning regimen. Every Friday morning at five a.m. the entire team would meet at our indoor track. Over the next hour, we were required to complete two-hundred-meter sprints in a specific time. As a wide receiver, our goal times were the fastest. The rest intervals were not long and seemed shorter and shorter with each sprint. The last thing any player wanted was to be singled out for not hitting their goal time, especially since this often led to the entire group redoing their sprint. Trash cans were spread out along the outside of the track as many of us needed them to vomit... or "rid ourselves of weaknesses," as the coaches called it, ha. As an underclassman I would finish near the front of the group on the first few sprints, then end the conditioning session near the rear. Things had to change. The conditioning couldn't be changed. I couldn't control the fitness levels of the players who finished in front of me. I needed that one degree of separation.

Over the next several months, after our mandatory early morning conditioning sessions, I would make my way over to the basketball arena. With the lights off and all alone, I would sprint up the stairs and walk down. The only sound was that of my panting echoing through the arena. When it came to improving my conditioning, that was my one-degree!

I had adopted that philosophy and applied it to every aspect of my life. I did all that was required and then more. The expectations I had for myself were greater than anyone else could prescribe. I wasn't satisfied with "good enough." I couldn't be. I was determined to maximize my potential. Anything short of that felt like failure. I was obsessed with that 212th degree. I needed the power of steam if I was to ever become a locomotive.

CYCLING IN THE SNOW

After graduating high school I enrolled at a community college outside of Portland, Oregon. My dad drove me down in a U-Haul and helped move me into my apartment, which was about a mile from campus. This was a very important detail, as I did not have a vehicle. I would either ride my bicycle or walk to class. My job at a pizza restaurant as a dishwasher was three miles away, and the rides home at night were often stressful and dangerous. I was very grateful for this job as it allowed me to have a personal pan pizza during my breaks. I did get a stern talking to by the manager when he found out I'd eaten a pizza that was sent back because it contained a wrong ingredient. I'd just discarded the slice that was bitten into, and ate the rest – waste not, want not, right? He disagreed, which made it a not-so-great night for me back in the dishwashing closet.

My roommate was a Japanese exchange student. He spoke very little English and I spoke no Japanese. Somehow, we communicated and had a lot of laughs. I learned about seaweed and rice... mainly that I didn't enjoy it and it smelled awful while being cooked!. He didn't have a car either, so we spent many days and nights just hanging out at home.

That year the temperatures dropped significantly by early December, and the snow soon followed. Each morning, my ride into class became more challenging and dangerous; the nights were even more precarious. Early one morning, I came up to a traffic signal. The red light, obviously, strongly advised me to stop; unfortunately, my bicycle did not receive that message. Upon locking my brakes and sliding on the ice, I began to peddle to gain some sort of traction. In a split second I decided to steer my bike off the road and into a ditch as opposed to oncoming traffic. I careened off the road, and laid in the snow on my back which was cushioned by my backpack. Embarrassed, I walked my bike the rest of the way to class. I needed to make a change.

I began looking through our local newspaper for a car (no, we didn't have the Internet to shop at that time) and found a brand new one. As I always do when making any large purchase, I called my mom. I sounded like a salesman as I pitched my idea of a car to her. I told her of my long hours at work and near-tragedies while attempting to get to class and that I had been able to save a thousand dollars from my dishwashing job. Surprisingly, she supported my idea. Looking back, I realize all I had to say was that her baby boy was risking his life! Ha.

Short shorts and no shirt with my first car.

I was in awe of this bright and shiny brand-new Honda Civic I found in the paper! The sticker listed the two-door coupe at nine thousand, nine-hundred and ninety-nine dollars. After putting down my one-thousand-dollar down payment, I was contractually obligated for the next five years. My payments were two-hundred-three dollars and twenty-six cents. Sounds like a pretty good deal, right? Think again. You see, my Civic was a five-speed. It did not have power steering. Apparently, the law didn't require vehicles to have a passenger-side rearview mirror because mine was non-existent. My luxurious Civic had a black plastic plate covering the slot where the radio should have been. I had no radio! None of these details bothered me. I was now protected from the elements and the threat of cars and ditches. I felt as though I was driving a Mercedes.

My payments ended just around the time I graduated college. I had no issues with it and eventually installed a radio and a CD player...I had it going on! I now owned my car outright. It was short-lived. After making the Dallas Cowboys, I sold her for five thousand dollars to a high school girl in my hometown of Snohomish, Washington. It had been a great five-year ride with the Green Machine, but now I felt ready to let her go and finally experience the joys of power steering.

ARE YOU HURT OR ARE YOU INJURED?

This is a common question from coaches, and you are programmed to provide only one answer: "Hurt." It sounds similar, but is vastly different if you understand the "code." Being "hurt" as opposed to "injured" means you are tough, you are strong, you put the team's needs before your own, that you'd prefer to play on a broken leg than miss a single play. It meant that you were a man and that the coaches could count on you. It was also quite possibly the hardest word a young guy had to force out of his mouth when what he really wanted to do was lay in the fetal position and be held by his mother. Too often during my career I was faced with that question and always answered it with, "I'm just hurt."

"Okay, good," the coach would say, "Stand up, stop moaning, and get back in the huddle." I would do as I was told, earning a slap on the butt for my efforts and proud that I had "taken one for the team." Over time this answer would be as automatic as breathing, even when I was too "hurt" to take a breath.

When injured, a player doesn't usually return to the game. In my more than one hundred games, I always returned. I never uttered the word "injured". So when I got knocked silly, my mom presumed I was fine, as did the coaches and the medical staff. Everything – our overall health, our playing time, and jobs – all hinged on the choice between those two words.

SECOND HALF

This section depicts some of the not-so-glamorous aspects of my time in the NFL – most of which involve my family, including having to leave my daughter to play in Europe. As far as my career goes, my head was above water, but at times, I still felt as though I was drowning.

NOPE, DON'T NEED YOU.

In a weird turn of events, after my third season, the Seahawks reached out to the Miami Dolphins inquiring about a potential trade for me. At that time, the Dolphins weren't willing to let me go. After my fourth season, as an unrestricted free agent, I told my agent I wanted to go home and play for the Seahawks. He reached out to them, and they said, "Nope, we don't have a need for him anymore." I guess I really *couldn't* go home again!

PRACTICE SQUAD TO SUPER BOWL

"Practice Squads" were comprised of an additional five players (separate from the fifty-three-man roster) who participate in all aspects of the team's practices and activities. They do not participate in games, however, and that – along with modest pay – is really all that distinguishes them from the others. While this seems like a tough gig, these athletes can be signed to any other team's Active Roster at any time during the season. In fact, this happened to my closest friend during my final year in the NFL in Baltimore, Maryland.

Now, this friend and I were inseparable. I remember us making up our own songs and performing them at open-mic events. During football practice I would hit him while jogging back to the huddle (and we were both on offense at the time). We'd make huge plates of macaroni and cheese nachos for dinner... the stories are endless. One of our weekly routines was going to the bank and deposit our checks. This was my fifth year in the NFL and his first year on the practice squad, so there was a big difference in the amount of our income. He gave me the hardest time, joking, "I work just as hard as you do and am not paid nearly what you are!" Well, the football gods must have heard his complaints. After fifteen weeks of this sort of banter, he was picked up out of the blue by another team and placed on their fifty-three-man roster. Not only did his pay significantly increase, but his new team won the Super Bowl that year. I finished my career a week later... he began his with a Super Bowl ring on his finger. Guess the joke was on me!

VIEW FROM BEHIND A LINEMAN'S BUTT

One of my jobs was returning punts and kicks; I would catch the ball and attempt to elude eleven men charging at full speed with intentions of running through my chest. Surprisingly, that wasn't the scariest moment for me. While I was playing with the Miami Dolphins, our starting quarterback was injured during a game. Later in the same game our backup QB also went down with an apparent injury. Back in the early 2000s, teams only suited up two quarterbacks, so out of nowhere, as if coming from God Himself, came the most terrifying command I'd heard in my football career: "Oggie, take some snaps, you're going in!" The Center (whose responsibility it is to hike the ball to the quarterback) grabbed me and we proceeded to take some practice snaps on the sideline. Had a TV been focused on me, the football-watching world would have undoubtedly seen my knees quivering with fear. I hadn't played QB since high school and had never taken ANY snaps since! That same voice, the one that seemed to come from God, said our backup was gonna be okay. Crisis averted. I look back on it now and wonder, what would've happened if I went into the game, threw a Hail Mary-type bomb, and scored a touchdown? But after careful consideration, if I could go back and relive that moment... I wouldn't change a damn thing!

ROOKIE DAZE...WORDS FROM A HALL OF FAME RUNNING BACK

"We can't get where we're trying to get if you can't get there!"

~ Emmitt Smith

I had just made the team as a Rookie. Emmitt Smith stopped me before heading out to our first practice on the Monday after the final cuts. While other things were said, I will never forget the moment he looked directly into my eyes and made the above proclamation. Essentially, he was reminding me that the Cowboys had a championship pedigree and there was an expectation for every team member – including me – to play at the highest level and compete for the Lombardi Trophy every year. Emmitt's words sunk in and I never rested on the fact that I had "made it" onto the team. It was my duty and my honor to continue to meet the standard that would "get us there" together.

Hazing of the Rookies

Contrary to some beliefs, no hazing took place that endangered another player...mostly because the team needed those rookies to help win games. Over the years I have seen rookies wrapped up with saran wrap and thrown into the ice tubs. Others had to stand up in the cafeteria and sing their college fight song. Since I was never expected to make the team, I avoided these embarrassments. Instead, after making the team, I was forced to carry in the veteran receivers' helmets after practice, then have bottles of Gatorade waiting for them at their locker. Thank goodness they were free.

In an unusual twist, I also became Larry Allen's "water boy." Larry was the most dominant offensive lineman the NFL has ever seen. Even in our wide receiver meetings, we would watch film of him blocking a defensive lineman clear into the bench on the sidelines.

I also remember all the players gathering around the weight room on physical testing day before the season began. All eyes were focused on Larry, laying on a bench underneath a barbell. On *each* side of this steel barbell were SIX forty-five-pound plates, plus a couple of smaller plates. All the players began to yell out words of encouragement. Larry took the barbell off the rack while the conditioning coach stood behind, ready to spot him if need be. He didn't need it. He lowered the steel barbell, which was now bent due to the amount of weight, down to his chest, then thrust it back up to its starting position. In total, he bench-pressed over six hundred pounds. Larry's strength was surpassed only by his speed and agility; *all* of his physical attributes were surpassed only by his humility and quiet demeanor.

Anyway, on the first day after practice I heard, in a very quiet and deliberate voice that seemed to lack some of the necessary consonants, "Oggie, go get me a Gatorade." In one of the best decisions of my life, I said, "Yessir." From that day on, I had a Gatorade waiting for all the wide receivers and three for Larry. In fact, I carried out Larry's directives even when I was no longer a rookie… and was honored to do so.

WHAT'S MY NAME?

I've pondered this question several times over the years. Ninety-nine percent of the team and coaches referred to me as "Oggie," short for Ogden. Deion Sanders, however, called me "Largent" – this, a reference to the Hall of Fame Seattle Seahawks' Wide Receiver, Steve Largent. He is considered to be one of the best players to play the position, not because he was the biggest or fastest receiver, but because of his impeccable route running. Since I was under no illusion that I was another Largent, I could only surmise that Sanders was comparing us because we shared the same skin color. In reality, he probably just called me that because he didn't know my real name, ha.

TEAM LUNCHEON DEBACLE

The Tuesday after final cuts there was the annual Cowboys luncheon. This would have been great, except for the fact that the only thing I'd brought to Dallas was my carry-on duffel containing some khaki shorts and few short-sleeved shirts. It had simply never occurred to me that I would be on the team after training camp. I also didn't have much money in the bank and wasn't due to receive my first check until after the first regular season game; nor did I have a vehicle. My options and resources were very limited, to say the least.

I convinced myself that I didn't need to get dressed up. It was just a luncheon – what's the worst that could happen? So I steamed my button-down, short-sleeved shirt with the steam from my shower, threw on my khaki cargo shorts and my fanciest (and only) pair of flip-flops.

I walked into the high-rise building in Uptown Dallas, where Cowboys' personnel showed me to a relatively small event room with twelve tables in close proximity to each other. When I saw some of my new teammates dressed in suits, I was mortified. I took my nametag and sat down at an eight-person table cover by white linen, thinking I would hide my body underneath the tablecloth. Maybe no one will notice, I thought, so long as I didn't stand or use the restroom. I was wrong.

When the rest of the team arrived, an announcement was made asking us to line up at the elevator so we could head up to the convention center. My eyes to the ground, I rose from my seat and went to stand in the crowded line of appropriately dressed Dallas Cowboys. They said nothing, and I thought I might come away from the event with some of my dignity intact. *Wrong again, Oggie.* We had no sooner piled into the service elevator when I heard a voice boom, "Largent!" I looked up to see Deion's incredulous appraisal. "What do you have on, Largent? Come on, man!" He then took off his baby blue, penguin-style suit jacket and told me to put it on. My ensemble now included brown sandals, khaki cargo shorts, a brown plaid short-sleeved shirt, and a custom suit jacket that probably cost five thousand dollars. Surprisingly, my humiliation evaporated; in fact, I was thoroughly pleased to be wearing Deion's jacket...and it fit!

Within seconds, that pleasure again turned into complete terror. The elevator doors slid open, and we filed out to form a line behind the wall of the convention center. Since I was number eighty-two, I had plenty of time to evaluate every decision I'd made in life that might have led me to this nightmare. I also had plenty of time to imagine the humiliation that lay ahead. At that moment, I felt it was my most difficult obstacle, ha.

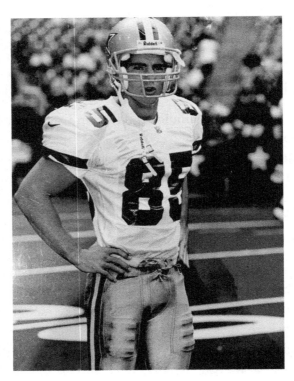

Hey Jeff, stop staring at the cheerleaders!

After about fifteen minutes, I approached the front of the line… and saw my fate. The grand ballroom was enormous, with at least fifty, twenty-person tables. Yes, folks, everything in Texas really IS bigger! The room was dark and music was playing in the background. Every major sponsor of the Dallas Cowboys was in attendance. Suddenly, I felt a hand gently clasp my arm. It was a gorgeous Cowboys Cheerleader, there to escort me to the stage. Wow…a dream and a nightmare rolled into one. The spotlight shined on us and the emcee announced my name, college, position, and jersey number. Most of the crowd cheered, but a few of the tables closest to the stage entrance stared me up and down, giggling. I suppose I should have been more embarrassed as I took my seat at the long linen table on the stage, but all I could think about was the wedding that cheerleader and I would one day have. Another dream, another obstacle I wouldn't overcome, ha.

Later, I relayed the story to my family and friends, who all found it highly entertaining. My accountant did not; the day following the luncheon he took me to Brooks Brothers to shop for suits and was kind enough to lend me the money for the two I picked out. I was now the sharpest-dressed broke man in all of Texas.

GAMEDAY

"OGGIE, WHAT THE HELL IS THAT?!"

During the fourth quarter of our final pre-season game, I took the hardest hit of my career to date. It happened as both teams were trying to wrap up the game and begin preparing for the first regular season game. On our final drive of the game, we faced a second and six. My route was a twelve-yard curl. The quarterback was being pressured and threw the ball several yards over my head. I gave it my best effort and leaped as high as I could, which unfortunately exposed my body to the other team's linebacker. He proceeded to ram the crown of his helmet directly into my lower back, a clean and vicious hit that knocked every bit of air from my lungs. I tested my limbs, grateful I could still feel them, rose to my feet and walked to the sidelines while seeing stars and struggling to breathe. I wanted to tap out, ring the bell, and hang up my cleats. I wanted to quit. Instead, I stood by the receiver's coach. After sitting out one play, he asked me if I was okay to go back in. It took everything I had to say yes. I went in for the final few run plays, counting the seconds until the clock ran out. Preseason was over, but my career would hang in the balance of the next few days as final cuts would be determined.

The following day, I noticed a baseball-sized growth had developed to the left of my spine above my left hip. With the final cuts looming, my only fear was that if the training staff saw this injury it would factor into their decision. I started wearing long t-shirts and avoided the medical staff at all costs.

Before I knew it, our first regular season game, versus the Arizona Cardinals, had arrived. I was so excited and nervous I didn't give much thought to the large mass on my back as I walked into the training room, dressed in shorts and a half-shirt, to warm up my legs in the whirlpool. As I was stepping into the water I heard our Head Trainer's voice call out, "Oggie, what the hell is that?" Caught off guard, my first thought was that I had unknowingly broken some game-day protocol. Had I mistakenly thought I could use the hot tub before the veterans? Did I violate a game-day superstition? Then the Head Trainer ordered me to come over and show him my back. Immediately, I began explaining that it only hurt when touched. Well, he didn't like that response and called the Team Doctor over to evaluate it. After I plead my case, and perhaps minimized the pain, they let me off with a warning. I was, however, to come in for treatment every day until they could reduce the swelling. I let out a sigh of relief and prepared to run out of the Dallas Cowboys tunnel to play, for the first time, in a REAL football game. The most amazing sequence of events happened during that game. Deion Sanders became a demi-god to me… and I was booed, for the first and only time, by a sold-out crowd at Texas Stadium.

Where you looking, Momma? It's game day. Let's focus!

"YES, DEION, WHATEVER YOU SAY, SIR!"

Allow me to set the stage. Deion Sanders, the most electric, athletic, fast, and skilled individual to ever play the game had just joined the Dallas Cowboys. The media staff had created a hype video to play on the huge screen directly above the field whenever Deion entered the game to return a punt, but the truth was, it wasn't necessary. There was always a palpable energy in the air every time he took to the field. During the second quarter of that first regular season game, Deion fielded a punt, made one player miss him, then spun three-hundred-sixty degrees to get crushed, head-on, by a Cardinal's defender. This brutal hit left Deion dazed as he staggered off to the sideline. Suspecting a concussion, the medical staff took him into the locker room, where he remained through halftime. I remember hearing Deion pleading with the doctors that he was fine and able to play in the second half. The doctors disagreed, and told him he'd have to sit the rest of the game out. I felt bad for him; the Cowboys had signed Deion to a huge contract, and I knew he didn't want to let the team or fans down. As our team left the locker room, walked through the tunnel, and onto our sidelines, my sympathy turned to a combination of excitement and nerves. With Deion benched, it would be my job to return punts for the rest of the game.

The Cardinals received the second-half kickoff and failed to gain a first down. We forced them to punt, so I ran onto the field to receive it. That's when I heard, "Largent! Largent... I got it, I got it!" and looked behind me to see Deion running through the tunnel and directly onto the field. I frantically ran off to the sidelines and overheard our team doctors and Special Team's Coach in a shouting match:

"WHY IS DEION OUT THERE? DID YOU TELL HIM THAT HE COULD PLAY?"

"I HAD NO IDEA...I DIDN'T TELL HIM ANYTHING!"

In the meantime, the play had begun and the punt was kicked. It spiraled high in the air, nearly hitting the video monitor that had played the Deion hype video just seconds earlier. Deion fielded the punt, made one defender miss, then another, then juked and sprinted by the other nine defenders to score a touchdown untouched and, more importantly, unharmed.

Deion walked off to the sideline while Texas Stadium erupted and shook with noise and cheers. He removed his helmet and declared in a conversational voice, "Now I'm done for the day." He then walked straight back up the tunnel and into the locker room from whence he came, leaving the mouths of the fans wide open in shock and awe. Chants of "Dei-on, Dei-on, Dei-on" resonated throughout the stadium. No longer was I just his teammate, I was his biggest fan. Although it was ninety degrees on the field, goosebumps covered my arms and neck. It was, and still to this day, remains the most "baller" thing I have ever witnessed.

With Deion back in the locker room, the punt-returning duties once again fell to me. Later in the third quarter, the Cardinals had to punt again. Immediately, the Deion hype video began to play. Instead of this demi-god running out, the crowd would instead see this unproven rookie run out onto the field. Boos rang out from the lower level to the nosebleed section. I stood out there, awaiting the punt, shaking my head in agreement. I, too, wished Deion was out there to amaze us again.

From that moment on, I looked to Deion for my orders whenever it came to returning punts. If he was winded from playing defense, he would look to me and issue directions. Without fail, in my mind, I would reply, "Yessir, Deion, whatever you say, sir!"

REALITY OF THE RULES, HEAD-TO-HEAD

It is not my intention to speak negatively about how we played the game twenty years ago. The rules and safety protocols were in place. Players, coaches, and medical staff operated under these guidelines. That said, there were no baselines back then when it came to concussions. There were also no rules against a defender launching himself into an offensive player with his head. Oftentimes, as a wide receiver and kick returner, I absorbed many of those hits to my head. However, two of them stand out most in my mind.

The first occurred while we were playing a home game against the Denver Broncos. I was lined up as a receiver nearest our sideline; my route, a modified "Go Route." This meant I was to run up the sideline, throttle down, and catch the ball twenty-five to thirty yards down the field. The ball was thrown perfectly over one defender (cornerback) and short of another (free safety) in their cover-two, scheme. As the ball arrived, so did the Bronco's safety. I failed to make the catch as his helmet made direct contact with mine. I "came to" staring at the turf, looking for my mouthguard. I remember hearing ooohs, ahhhhs, and then a team-mate yelled, "Oggie, your teeth!" I immediately rubbed my tongue to the bottom of my upper teeth; they were intact, but several chips of my teeth lay on the turf. "Concussion protocol" at that time consisted of one question: "Can you go back in?" And of course, my answer was yes.

The other occurred a season later when I was playing with the Miami Dolphins. I entered the game to return a punt. I received the ball and began sprinting up the field. After juking a couple of would-be tacklers, I faced a defender that I was unable to avoid. Instinct took over and I lowered my head in anticipation of the inevitable collision. The tackler had the same thoughts. Our helmets met while both going nearly full speed. I arose from the tackle, dazed and confused, as I did after most punt returns. I stumbled to the sideline and felt that my helmet no longer fit properly. Something was wrong. At the time I believed it to be my ear pads. I felt one pressing onto my face nearest to my left eye. The other earpad was pressed against my head behind my right ear. I voiced my concern to our equipment manager on the sideline. After a quick examination, he stated, "In all my years, I have never seen this happen!" It turned out, that during that tackle, I had bent the steel facemask, which made my helmet oblong – a distinction I didn't care to have. "Can you still play, Oggie?" the trainers asked.

"Yep."

INSTANT REPLAY: MOM, I'M FINE!

One of my biggest concerns as a professional football player was my family, in particular my mom. Like the vast majority of mothers, she didn't enjoy seeing her children suffering or in pain. Knowing this would be an issue throughout my career, early on I adopted a channel of communication that was meant only for her. As mentioned earlier, in a college game versus our biggest rival, the Idaho Vandals, I was knocked unconscious.

That incident had my entire family on the edge of their seats, and as I lay motionless on the field I promised my mom to never get hurt again. While I failed to keep that promise, I told my mom that I would

MOM, I'M FINE

Jeff Ogden, who played at Snohomish High School, returns punts for the Miami Dolphins. Even though he's good at returning kicks, his mother worries about him. She knows her son has a dangerous job, and Sunday she'll see him play live in the NFL for the first time when Miami plays the Seahawks at Husky Stadium. After every punt return, the son will tap his helmet to let his mother know he's okay. Even when that's not true.

acknowledge her after every hit on the football field. I began to softly knock on the top of my helmet with my fist. Before I returned any kick or punt, and after every tackle, I would go through this routine. At times, even after being knocked out in one way or another, I would eventually stand up and knock on my head to signal, "Mom, I'm fine."

NO SICK "DAZE": I THINK I BROKE MY COLLAR BONE

Other than the repeated hits to my head, I only had one other significant injury during my NFL career. I was returning a punt against the New York Jets during the fifth game of the 2001 season. After fielding the punt and gaining a few yards, I was tackled by a defender – a big, strong fella. The tackle was relatively gentle, but I landed on the ground with all of his weight on top of me. I heard a pop, and when I stood up I realized I couldn't move my arm at all. I walked slowly off the field with my right arm hanging limp at my side. A team trainer met me when I approached the sideline and asked me what was wrong. "I think I broke my collarbone," I replied in a very brave, calm manner and not showing any distress. Injuries were just part of the job, but the pain isn't something you can prepare for. I just had to accept it, fix it, and not cry. Ha.

The team doctors examined my collarbone underneath my shoulder pads and determined that my collarbone was intact; the popping was just my shoulder dislocating. Phew! They escorted me off the field early in the second quarter and back to the locker room. They cut my jersey off and gently removed my shoulder pads. Any movement I had in my right shoulder was accompanied by intense pain. I received several numbing shots with small needles. Then came the big boy! The thickest and longest needle I had ever seen was injected into my shoulder joint. The medical trainers then massaged my shoulder and moved my arm around – I assumed to "lubricate" the joint. After a couple of minutes passed, they instructed me to lift my arm above my head and to my amazement I was able to do it. I laughed, thinking what a "miracle" this was – just moments earlier I hadn't been able to move my arm at all. The trainers cut a small pad and taped it to the underside of my shoulder pads. I put them on along with a new jersey. "Have a good second half, Oggie!" WHAT?!?!

I finished that game having to make some drastic modifications. Although I could now move my right arm, it moved verrrry slowly. This unfortunate reality forced me to use my left arm to wave above my head to call for a fair catch and also carry the ball in my left hand. Anyone who thinks that sounds simple ought to try writing with their non-dominant hand. I can tell you playing football that way is much, much worse.

HALFTIME ON THE TOILET

Playing in the NFL has many perks. One of them is always having medical staff available. Morning, noon, and night, we had amazing staff that would tend to injuries, treatments, and illnesses. I needed and took full advantage of their expertise nearly every day of my five-year career. There is one regret I have, however, stemming from an event that occurred in Indianapolis.

It was the day before our game against the Colts, and I was not feeling well. My naïve approach to the situation was to drink Gatorade and eat a few good meals leading up to the game. The food and proper hydration failed me. I spent that evening walking back and forth from my bed to the bathroom. Once my body purged every ounce of fluid and nutrient from my system, I was able to get around two hours of sleep. I didn't call our medical staff because I didn't want to interrupt their sleep, ha. Big mistake. I remember waking up with abs so sore I felt as though I'd been punched in the gut. I also remember considering tucking up my jersey because I thought they looked very defined, ha.

That morning, after explaining my restless night to the trainers, they administered some anti-nausea pills. I did all I could to nibble at breakfast and keep down any fluids. These treatments helped… a little.

Our team buses arrived at the Indianapolis Colts Stadium two hours prior to kickoff. With my pale face, weak muscles, and defeated mind, I immediately checked in with the medical training staff. My weight was significantly lowered as dehydration had set in, and I knew I couldn't participate in the game. The training staff had me lay on a table and proceeded to administer an IV bag to my left and right arms simultaneously. Even during that time, it was hard for me to not run to the bathroom stalls. As tough as it was to admit, I was in no shape to play; I was just lying there, hoping to survive. When I told the training staff how badly I was feeling, they seemed to understand, but a few minutes later, as fluids were still coursing through my veins, the owner of our team, Jerry Jones, approached me. He held onto my wrist and, genuinely concerned, asked me how I was feeling. I told him, "Not good." He then saddled up next to me on the training table, half-sitting on it and half-standing. "Let me tell you a story..." he began. The owner, the man who signs my paychecks, recounted a time during his playing days in college. His teammate, who was first-string, wasn't able to play in a game due to an injury. Mr. Jones, the second-string player, got his chance to play, played well, and started every game after that. After telling me that story, he let go of my wrist, stood up, patted me on the shoulder and said, "Have a great game out there, son." Any indecision about whether or not I would play that day vanished with those seven words. I went out there for the first half and played as hard as I could...but the second half was a different story.

At halftime, the team filed into the locker room. During this time, players would seek any required medical treatment, repair any equipment malfunction, eat snacks, and hydrate before the coaching staff addressed the team. None of this applied to me. As soon as I entered the locker room doors, I raced to the bathroom stalls. Surely, our twenty-minute halftime would allow me to "get right" so I could finish the game. As it turned out, I needed twenty-five minutes, ha. We were scheduled to receive the second-half kickoff. I was our starting kick returner, and I hadn't been able to leave the bathroom yet, which left our coaching staff confused. Several minutes later, embarrassed, I jogged across the field and onto our sidelines. I felt like all eyes were on me. I imagined the announcers chuckling. None of that mattered as I just prayed I didn't have an "accident" if I got hit too hard on National TV. Thankfully, I didn't, and I can proudly say I have never missed a game due to injury or illness over the course of my career.

BYE, BABY GIRL...I'M LEAVING FOR EUROPE

Uncertainties are commonplace in the NFL. Sicknesses, trades, and injuries happen every day. I accepted those risks, but was not prepared for this one!

In the winter of 2000, after my second year in the NFL, I learned that the Cowboys were going to allocate me to play in NFL Europe. This was a great opportunity to polish my skills and gain valuable playing experience — experience I had not gained during my short career. Training camp for NFLE took place in Orlando, Florida. We spent three weeks practicing before flying over to Germany where we would begin our ten-game season. There was only one issue with this assignment: my daughter was due to be born while I was in Orlando at training camp.

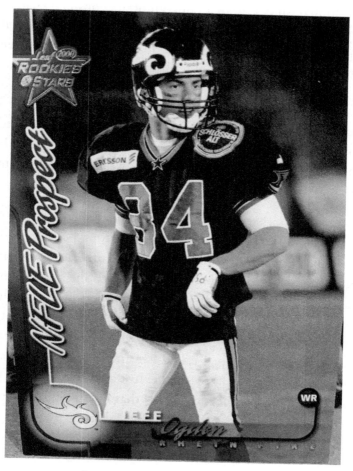

'PSO' on gloves honoring my baby girl

The doctors agreed to schedule an inducement so I could fly back to Dallas and witness the birth, but I would have only twenty-four hours before returning to my team. I arrived in Dallas on the morning of March 20 and took a taxi straight to the hospital. The medicine had already been administered to speed up the process. Several hours later, my seven-pound baby girl was born. She had baby acne and hair all over her head and was the most beautiful sight I had ever seen. We named her Peytan Starr.

With my limited time, I sat in an uncomfortable hospital chair and held her as often as they'd let me. I never slept. During one of my breaks from admiring my daughter, I called my agent and my mom, and emphatically stated that I was not going to return to my team. I was going to quit football. I was not going to leave my daughter. My momma, as only she can do, explained to me the benefits my career could have for Peytan. I wanted to hear none of it. Nothing else in the world mattered to me that night. All I could see, all I could feel, was a love like none I had ever experienced. Nothing – not even football – was going to keep me from the greatest love of my life.

In the end, my mother, and logic, won out. She reminded me that two more years in the NFL would qualify me for a pension and several other financial benefits; it would also provide other opportunities and open doors that otherwise would be shut to me. She also reminded me that I could see Peytan all the time. She and others in my family would fly her out to watch my games every week. She pointed out that I could spend the six months of my off-seasons with her. After several hours of deliberation and no sleep, I called her and my agent back and told them I would continue with my career. Just a few days later, I boarded an aircraft bound for Europe, devastated that I would have to spend the next three months halfway around the world from the tiny baby girl who had become my heart.

All smiles after flight to Düsseldorf, Germany.

Was it worth it? Yes. My family was able to bring her over to Europe for a week. (God bless them for flying thirteen hours with a newborn... and everyone else on that flight!) I kept my daughter in my hotel room the night after our game. I had a headache, as I usually did after games, and Peytan apparently had some "jetlag" as demonstrated by her unwillingness to sleep and incessant crying. I made several calls to the adjacent hotel room where my mom and dad were staying inquiring about how to help my baby girl sleep. Knowing I was pretty beat-up from the game, Mom offered to come take her, but I declined the loving offer and accepted her advice instead. It was a restless night to say the least, but I wanted to remember every second with Peytan. In fact, while she was with me that night, she left me a reminder that I still keep to this day. Her belly button thingy fell off! I immediately put it in a container. Yeah, I know it's weird. I guess that's more proof of how hard I was hit during that game a few hours prior! Ha.

Every parent, grandparent, etc. makes great sacrifices for their loved ones. My family's support and help were invaluable. I made a difficult decision the night I decided to continue playing professional football. It was the first of many. In the end, football provided me and Peytan with memories we will never forget. And if we do forget, we will always have this book to refresh them.

TRADE DAZE

Inevitably, if one plays long enough, he will experience this side of the business. There are a million factors that go into making this difficult decision by the team staff. I can't imagine anyone taking joy in this necessary evil, and I won't go into the multitude of reasons it qualifies as such, but here is my experience with being traded.

In the fall of 2000, I returned from playing in NFL Europe, an experience I was grateful to have. I had developed and learned a great deal; I had also been named "All-World" and earned a World Bowl Championship – all this despite being injured in the seventh game of the ten-game season. I suffered a torn muscle in the arch of my foot, severe ankle sprain, and "turf toe" – a sprain of the ligaments around the big toe. Essentially, that portion of my body was rendered useless. This is not an easy injury to come back from as a wide receiver.

Though it wasn't a popular decision to make, I refused the NFL mandate of returning to the U.S. to rehabilitate my injuries. In my mind, I had been sent overseas to become a more polished receiver and contribute to a World Championship. Somehow, the owner of the Cowboys, Jerry Jones, persuaded the powers-that-be to allow me to stay and finish what

Giving my helmet to this little boy cost me $225, ha!

I had started. No surprise there – Mr. Jones always seemed to get what he wanted. In a show of great support, he flew to Germany to watch me and a few other teammates play in the World Bowl.

Mr. Jerry Jones congratulating the team after World Bowl Championship

I spent the next two weeks rehabbing my ankle and foot day and night. I would vomit daily with the stationary bike workouts. I would ingest highly oxygenated calves' blood capsules to aid in muscle recovery. I spent hours in an oxygen-deprivation chamber to accelerate the healing process. (I'm pretty sure this wasn't an approved treatment in the States.)

The night of the World Bowl Championship was the first live action I had seen in twenty-one days. With my toe, foot, and ankle heavily taped, and with pain meds numbing them all, I ran out of the tunnel patting my head to let my mom, who was in attendance, know I was okay. I wasn't – in my estimation, I was operating at about only sixty percent – but I had sacrificed too much to not play in the most important game of the season.

With just seconds left on the clock, the World Bowl Championship game came down to one play. I knelt on a knee, in tears, praying, and listening to the crowd scream as the opposing team's kicker was about to attempt a game-winning field goal. The ball was kicked. My teammate, who was clinching my arm at the time, jumped up and began screaming with joy. I, however, kept my eyes closed and remained on my knee. So many emotions came to my mind – my daughter, my family, my team, and most of all, God. By this time, the adrenaline had worn off and I could barely walk. I hobbled onto the field to hug my teammates, coaches, and anyone else I could find. Soon after, I met my parents, brother and sister-in-law, and Mr. Jones on the field. With a firm embrace he said, "You did it, Jeff, congratulations!" Learning from our previous embarrassing conversations, and the realization that nothing I had ever accomplished was on my own, I simply responded, "Yes sir, WE did!"

Just six weeks later, I would be traded to the Miami Dolphins.

A player is usually the last person to know about the fate of his career. I'm not complaining, but we are at times just a simple business commodity. I knew all of that going into this line of work, and I'm perfectly okay with it. That doesn't mean it's not incredibly inconvenient, to say the least.

During the spring of 2000, while I was playing in NFL Europe, the Dallas Cowboys had made coaching changes, including an entirely new offense. I would be returning from Europe with a lot to learn, and, I felt, at a disadvantage, so I was eager to heal, get back on the field, and begin to show I was worthy of a roster spot. This was shaping out to be another difficult obstacle both physically and mentally. I had no idea that it was going to be as tough as it was.

I had been rehabilitating my injury throughout the summer and into the fall Training Camp. A new batch of rookies and free-agent veterans were hungry to make the team. I knew this and became increasingly frustrated with each passing day that I was unable to participate. If I couldn't be on the field, I couldn't prove myself. If I couldn't prove myself, I couldn't contribute to the team. My frustration grew into desperation as the preseason began and I was still sidelined with this injury from Europe. Knowing that the likelihood of me making the final roster was shrinking, I resorted to desperate measures. I began to exaggerate my progress and downplay the pain. I was constantly questioned by the media about my return. My answers became shorter and shorter. My responses were more direct and emphatic, "I feel good. I'm ready to go." Then I lost my mind and forced the issue a bit, ha.

During an afternoon practice in front of thousands of fans and a host of reporters, I walked out onto the practice field while the team was stretching. It was a hundred degrees and the attire for that practice was just helmets…no pads. I, however, chose to ignore that memo, ha. Eyes began looking in my direction as I proudly walked onto the practice field dressed in full gear: shoulder pads, game pants, helmet and cleats. Then, in front of the spectators, and with my mouthpiece in, I very firmly mumbled to the trainers that I was going to practice! After their shock wore off and they stopped laughing, they set me straight. "No, you're not, Oggie. Now let's get started on your rehab drills." Whelp, at least I tried.

That little "show" satisfied my need to be heard; however, it wasn't necessary. Unbeknownst to me, the Cowboys were working on a trade with the Miami Dolphins. While a trade is being discussed, the last thing either team wants is for the player to get injured for any reason. I had been held out of practice to ensure I was healthy. In the end, the Dolphins got me, and I think the Cowboys just got a case of Gatorade or something, ha.

I was informed of the trade following practice, as was the media. After meeting with Mr. Jones, I was told my flight would be leaving that evening for Miami, Florida. At this time, I owned a home and my daughter was just four months old. I gave a couple interviews thanking the Jones family for an amazing opportunity before hurrying to my car. I had to pack up my life and get my affairs in order within a few hours. Oh yeah, and I would be playing a game, with a new team, in just two days. I didn't even know my new quarterback's name!

Being traded was not the end of the world. In fact, it was just another world. A world that enabled me an opportunity to continue playing the game I love...a way to provide for my family and daughter... a way to impact children's lives, give back to the community, and share my faith. I was, and still am, extremely grateful to the Cowboys Organization for taking a chance on an unknown twenty-three-year-old kid, for giving me the valuable experience to play in NFL Europe, and for opening another door in Miami when mine was closing in Dallas.

TIMEOUT: HEAD THROUGH A BRICK WALL

"For me life is continuously being hungry. The meaning of life is not simply to exist, to survive, but to move ahead, to go up, to achieve, to conquer."

~Arnold Schwarzenegger

A common quote is, "When one door closes, another one opens." It's a cute sentiment, but in my opinion a bit too passive. I prefer to think that doors only open when knocked upon or knocked down. We're all going to face obstacles and it's up to us to be proactive in overcoming them. We're also going to experience setbacks, and the greatest challenge will be to not allow feelings of defeat to rob us of focus. I see setbacks more of a pause – a time to get back in the huddle and catch my breath before continuing my journey. During these times, I must accept "what is," maintain my focus on what I want "it" to be, and construct ways to face the setback head-on. "The shortest distance between you and your goal is determined by the length of time you give your setback." -Jeff Ogden, 2021 Ha.

CHALK TALK

Given your specific goals, what can you do when faced with a setback to overcome or navigate around obstacles? Having a "growth mindset" means that hard work yields possibilities, rather than limitations. List five things that you feel you cannot do, struggle with, or hold you back. Now add the word "yet" at the end of each statement of "impossibilities." Do you see how this one word shifts your perspective? Continue this practice in all your self-talk or whenever you come up against those limitations.

POST-SEASON

As you saw in the previous section, I dealt with many trials, tribulations, and hard knocks (literally) over the course of my NFL career. I also have been fortunate enough to be recognized for some achievements, have been able to use them for good, and even exploited them for reality TV. I offer some of those light-hearted stories to you here.

MY FIRST NFL TOUCHDOWN

After being traded before the beginning of my third NFL season, I began a new chapter with the Miami Dolphins. My body was about seventy percent healthy, as my foot and toe were still recovering from injuries sustained in NFL Europe. My role with the Dolphins would be the same – a backup wide receiver for all positions; I would also participate on several special teams. My mindset remained, "the more you can do."

The punt-returning duties were assigned to a very a capable receiver when I signed with the Dolphins. He was fast, elusive, and had great hands. When our punt-return team required two returners, I would join my teammate. My job would be to lead-block for him after ensuring he was able to catch the ball without getting his head knocked off. Needless to say, he loved it when I was out there. I would be the only punt returner back to receive punts when a "fair catch" was more likely going to happen. This occurs when the opposing team is around midfield and they attempt to kick the ball inside our ten-yard line. Ninety-nine percent of the time, this called for a "fair catch," which allowed me to catch the punt without getting my own head knocked off and let our offense begin from that position. The coaches trusted me to make good decisions back near our own goal line, and successfully secure the ball. I was not the type of returner who would try to juke tacklers, run side-to-side or risk losing yards on the return. I wasn't Deion Sanders. I was seen as a player whose only purpose was to transition the ball over to our offense and let the real athletes perform. (Most viewers at home would be taking a bathroom break during these plays, ha.)

Every football play is scripted and has a purpose, but that doesn't mean they play out that way. In our third game of the 2000 season, we were playing the Baltimore Ravens on a Sunday night when their scripted punt did not play out as expected. I was in the game with my other receiver prepared to just be his lead-blocker. The Raven's punter kicked the ball, and it came off the side of his foot a little bit. This caused the ball to fly in the opposite direction of his desired intention. It left me with no choice but to catch it. After yelling, "I got it, I got it!" I received the ball and scampered thirty-one yards before being tackled. It was the right play at the right time. We were able to score a touchdown and went on to win the game 19-6.

For our eighth game that season, we hosted Brett Favre and the Green Bay Packers. There were 73,740 spectators at Pro Player Stadium on this gorgeous Sunday afternoon in late October. The Packers had jumped out to a 17-7 lead at halftime. It was a very competitive and hard-fought battle offensively and defensively. The difference, ultimately, turned out to be our special teams.

When our offense stalled in the third quarter, our coaches needed a spark and resorted to their bag of tricks. We were lined up in our punting formation around our own forty-yard line. Instead of snapping the ball back to our punter, we snapped it to the running back. We called a fake punt! Our running back rambled up the field, gained the first down, and put our offense in great field position. Our offense took full advantage of the opportunity and scored a few plays later. We trailed 17-14. We then took the lead 21-17 approaching the fourth quarter. After our defense was able to stop Bret Favre's offense with around seven minutes left to play in the game, the Packers' punt team took the field. Since it was a "fair-catching" situation, I jogged onto the field to fulfill my duties of waving my hand above my head for a fair catch. Well, like I said earlier, football doesn't always play out as planned.

I stood back at our ten-yard line and waited for the punt. To everyone's surprise, the snapper for the Packers hiked the ball too high and the punter had to jump just to catch it. This threw off the timing of his kick. In an attempt to just get the punt off, he was forced to speed up his kicking process.

The punt didn't reach its normal altitude or travel its designed distance, which left me in a precarious position. Football analytics, football fans, and any rational individual would say, "Get the hell out of the way and let the ball bounce!" As the ball flew relatively low to the ground, there were Packer defenders sprinting all around me. At this moment, I had two options: one: wave my hands over my head and safely catch the ball or two: get my head knocked off. My fight-or-flight response kicked in, and the "fight" won out, which in this case meant making a play on the ball.

I saw the ball traveling in my direction. As it got closer, more defenders surrounded me. I, like many times prior, decided to sacrifice my safety and attempt to catch the ball. I understood that I would take a big hit; my only thought was not to fumble the ball while absorbing that hit. Somehow, I caught the punt and began to run. I made a few tacklers miss me, and then, just like driving through a tunnel, I came out the other side. No Packer defender had touched me. The only thing left in front of me was eighty-one yards to the end zone. I just had to breathe, not pull a muscle, not freak out, not drop the ball, not trip over my own feet, and outrun everyone to score, ha. A convoy of my teammates ran alongside me as I scored my first NFL touchdown!

TIMEOUT: PRIDE COMES *WITH* THE FALL

"To whom much is given, much will be required" (Luke12:48). Operating with the understanding that your "ego" is your "self," one can identify in many ways. My identity has been formed over the past four decades. I have experienced the humblest of times, and periods of pride. I have been denied entry into our team hotel, and have witnessed fans cry over my autograph. I have been confronted with both sides of my identity as an adult. Much has been given to me, and I intend to fulfill my requirements of helping and giving back to others.

CHALK TALK

How and what is your service to others? What are you prideful of, and is it healthy pride or ego-based? ? How can you humble yourself daily?

SHOWDOWN WITH TOM BRADY... *kinda*

My only regular-season touchdown reception as a wide receiver occurred against the 2002 Super Bowl champions, the New England Patriots. It was a frigid evening at Foxboro Stadium in late December, there was one minute, twenty-eight seconds left on the clock and, once again, my destiny loomed in the balance. After breaking the huddle, I lined up at the receiver position. When the ball was snapped, I beat my defender, leaped high in the air, and landed on my back in the end zone...TOUCHDOWN! I had successfully and single-handedly impacted the G.O.A.T's career!

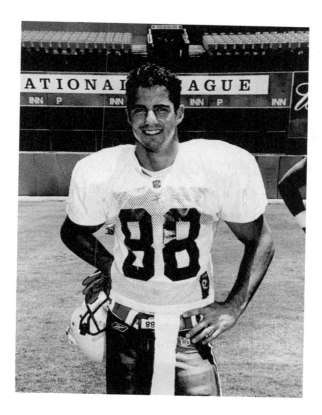

In reality, it was nowhere near that exciting. In fact, that touchdown was meaningless to everyone except my family and myself, ha. We were losing by two touchdowns at the time and the game was, for all intent and purposes, over. I'm sure our coaches just told our quarterback to "give the lil' kid a chance." I had imagined, planned, and even practiced my "touchdown dance" several times over the years. "What are you gonna do if you score?" was a common question I got from friends. *I thought it would be hilarious if I scored, ran toward the goalpost, attempted to dunk the ball over the post, not jump high enough, get rejected by the post, and fall on my back. No doubt, I would be immortalized on every sports blooper reel and therefore have irrefutable proof of my football career, ha.* Instead, my lone touchdown reception came at a time in the game when fans were exiting the stadium, broadcasters were talking about next week's games, and TV viewers were changing the station to watch 60 Minutes. So, no celebration occurred, no dance, no failed attempt at dunking the football over the goal post. I succeeded at living out a dream of catching a pass for a touchdown, But the score was now, Jeff Ogden – 1, Tom Brady – 581…a slight edge to the Greatest of All Time.

INSTANT REPLAY: THE MECCA-LAMBEAU FIELD

I was fortunate enough to play in all thirty-one NFL football stadiums during my career. The old Texas Stadium held most of my memorable moments, including my first game, first catch, first tackle… and first fumble, ha.

Before every game, I would head out to the field with a quarterback to go through a pre-game warm-up. I would put on some shorts, t-shirt, and my receiver gloves, but no cleats or socks. Shoes in general restricted my feet and caused great discomfort – a residual effect of my foot issues as a child – so I preferred to run through my warmup routine barefoot. I loved the feeling of the short, manicured turf under my toes.

It was during these pre-game warmups that I felt happiest, most alive, and could take in the magnitude of what playing professional football was all about. Those feelings would leave me when it came time to go through our scheduled, full pads and cleats warmups.

There was one stadium that stood out among all the others: Lambeau Field. My only opportunity to play in Green Bay was during a preseason game, and I was as excited for it as I had been for the five playoff games I had played in over my career. When we arrived, my feelings of awe were confirmed. Lambeau Field was not the largest stadium or the loudest, but you would never know that while standing on the sidelines or on the field. The stands were as close to the sidelines as possible. We could hear every conversation, every heckle, and every derogatory word – some were actually clever and I couldn't help but laugh.

The grass, as I ran across it during my pre-game ritual, felt heavenly on my bare feet. It was so soft and comfortable to fall on, it almost made me want to get tackled, ha. This was going to be our final pre-season game, and I had already secured my spot on the final roster for the season. This meant that I would only see a little playing time to ensure injuries wouldn't occur. The only play I remember is returning a punt. I caught the punt and made the first few tacklers miss. I scampered around forty yards before being knocked out of bounds. For some reason, I was smiling and laughing the whole way. I was having fun, enjoying myself, and taking in the historic environment.

It was a pre-season game, meant nothing in the grand scheme of things, and I can't remember ninety-nine percent of the actual game. To me, however, it was everything I'd thought it would be and more. The gift to play at the "un-frozen tundra of Lambeau Field" will forever be ingrained in my memory!

CELEBRITY STUFF

THE OTHER SIDE OF AN AUTOGRAPH

One of the craziest things about playing in the NFL was signing autographs. Sure, I had seen plenty of players do this – just a year earlier *I* had been asking for autographs at the Seahawks training camp, which was held at my university where I worked as a security guard. Yet, some- how, it was a "part of the job" I never anticipated. In college, most of my professors didn't know my name. Now, at training camp, hundreds of fans stood alongside a fence after practice, hoping players, including me, would stop and sign their footballs or pictures.

The weather was brutally hot during training camp, we were tired, and all we could think about was Gatorade and the meal waiting for us. Sign- ing autographs after practice was sometimes the last thing we wanted to do. So I was pleasantly surprised, and moved, to see so many of our star players stop and make a child's day.

I resolved then and there that I would provide an autograph to anyone who sought one. If I could help that fan's day be more enjoyable, it was the least I could do. A brilliant aspect of being a professional foot- ball player is that we are afforded many opportunities to uplift spirits. It didn't matter if it happened from the field or at a church, school, fund- raiser, or hospital – it was by far the most enjoyable aspect for me.

> One particular autograph brought that "joy" close to home. My dad purchased an autographed eight-by-ten photo of me at a charity auction. He paid two-hundred and seventy-five dollars for it, then promptly asked *me* to give him the money! My response: "Nope!" That photo still hangs in his hall along with several other photos that I gave him... for free.

CELEBRITY SIGHTING STORIES

I often laugh when thinking about how people reacted when "spotting" me out in public. One of the differences between today's NFL and when I was playing is the number of cameras used to document the games. Back when I played, there were maybe a few. Today, there are sideline cameras, rolling towers, rafter cameras, on-field cameras held up by wires, and bench cameras that capture every intimate detail. Snap cadences are easy to hear, and dialogue between players is very clear. And then of course there are fans with cell phones clutched in their hands, always ready to take a picture or video and post it to social media. This did not exist during my time, and for the most part players remained hidden by helmets and shoulder pads. Back then, players were recognized in one of two ways: their product endorsements or massive size. I did not fit into either of those categories; I was a six-foot-one, one-hundred ninety-five pounds and, other than my overly thick neck, a pretty average-looking dude. The last thing people would guess was that I played professional football, not even, as it turned out, when I was sitting right next to them!

One Tuesday afternoon my dad and I were at the Grapevine Mills Mall and decided to have lunch at Chili's. We bellied up to the bar next to two men and couldn't help overhearing that they were talking about the Cowboys — a very common occurrence in Texas during the fall. Suddenly, I heard my name and glanced at my dad, amused at the look of shock on his face. I put my index finger to my lips to stop him from saying anything to them, then we intently listened in. Fortunately, nothing negative was spoken of me. I just thought it was funny — and a little odd — to be the topic of their conversation and completely anonymous at the same time.

I even had the NFL gaming world fooled. My oldest sister Andrea is an elementary school teacher in my hometown of Snohomish, Washington. One morning, as she was explaining the day's lesson, a young boy raised his hand to ask a question. Imagine Andrea's surprise when he asked, "Mrs. Ogden, is your brother black?" Laughing, she asked why he had thought that. He replied, "I was playing Madden Football on my PlayStation last night. I chose the Cowboys as my team and your brother came up as a black man!"

The Chili's story was not unusual; in fact, I probably could have gone almost anywhere in public while wearing my jersey without being recognized. This made my occasional stalking experiences even stranger. Instead of approaching me, introducing themselves, or asking for an autograph, some people would begin to follow me. In stores, they would creep around the racks of clothes… walk at what they thought was an inconspicuous distance behind me, or eavesdrop and whisper at adjacent booths at restaurants. In one case, a car followed me while I was driving. I was forced to take a detour. When I was sure I was being followed, I confronted the driver at a traffic light. When I asked him if he was following me, he replied, "Do you want me to?" I responded by pressing the gas pedal to the floor.

By far, the most attention I received was when I was on The Millionaire Matchmaker. I was living in Austin at the time of the premiere, and suddenly it seemed every woman in town knew who I was. They would approach me and without preamble start spouting things about my life as if we were old friends…or more. I also received messages from women all across the United States and foreign countries as well. Some sent kind messages; others were promoting themselves as someone who would "love me." Still others were family members, including moms, selling their daughters attributes'. (I won't even get into some of the photographs I received.) Needless to say, all this was awkward and sometimes unnerving. Then one day I parked outside a coffee shop and was about to walk in. Across the street, I heard an, "Oh My God, that's Jeff Ogden!" from a woman who was standing with her significant other. I smiled and waved at them, and after I got over that initial feeling of embarrassment, I felt like a real celebrity for the first time!

My life as a "celebrity" was relatively short-lived. I felt like I got to experience how the one percent lived for a while. I never got caught up in any of it and found it amusing that a regular boy from Snohomish, Washington could receive this star treatment.

CATCH A STAR FOUNDATION

One of the best things about being in the NFL was that it gave me a platform from which I could positively affect lives. Sometimes this happened in rather unorthodox ways, like when I was involved in a Valentine's Day charity auction and a man bid $11,500 for me to take his significant other on a date.

A more sustainable and philanthropic opportunity came soon after. My degree is in Special Education, so from the beginning I knew I wanted to create a foundation that would help children. As had happened many other times in my life, I prayed for, and received, clarity on this goal. One day my brother Pat told me about some friends who weren't able to have children due to some medical issues. They had looked into adoption and were disheartened to learn it carried a hefty price tag – about twenty-five thousand dollars, most of which would go toward attorney's fees. This couple, both teachers, did not have that kind of money at their disposal.

I began researching the adoption process and learned some startling facts. There were more than one hundred thousand children in foster care who were looking for a permanent home, and thousands of individuals looking to adopt. Many of them, like Pat's friends, would have made excellent parents but were prevented from doing so because of the financial obstacles. That's when the idea for The Catch a Star Foundation was born. Over the next three years, we were able to place two children in homes and provide educational scholarships for others. The numbers may not sound staggering, but we made an incredible impact on the families involved. I am humbled that my ability to catch a football enabled me to help others, and I'm eternally grateful for my staff and board of directors – none of whom took a salary – for making it happen.

TIMEOUT – SPARE CHANGE

Providing entertainment is great, but doesn't last. I believe the greatest gift is to make a more permanent difference in the lives of others. I wasn't able to have a twenty-year career in the NFL, but there is no timeline on how long I may be able to positively affect the lives of others because of it.

CHALK TALK

What are you passionate about? Write down some options to volunteer, or give back to a cause you believe in. Before reading any more of this book, call to schedule an appointment with the "cause" of your choice.

_____

_____

_____

_____

_____

_____

_____

_____

_____

_____

_____

_____

_____

_____

_____

_____

_____

_____

_____

_____

_____

OFF-SEASON

"Forgive your younger self. Believe in your current self. Create your future self."

This section is the most important reason why I chose to write this book. There have been several times in my journey when I believed my life was not worth living and, with a spirit of vulnerability, I share some of them here in the hope that my struggles will positively impact a life or two.

MY FOREVER OFF-SEASON

I like to think of life as a series of seasons, constantly moving forward, never slowing down for any reason or anyone. Each season has its own obstacles, challenges, and setbacks; each has its own joys, victories and accomplishments. In the many seasons of my life I have certainly experienced my share of them all — something I often reflect on during this, what I refer to as my "forever off-season." As I mentioned in the introduction of this book, I want to be transparent about the obstacles I am currently facing and how I am navigating and living with them. I want to first paint a picture of my struggles and follow up with my attempt at tackling them. I have chosen to not just be alive, but to live!

BRAIN TRAUMA DRAMA

Undoubtedly, the following pages have been the toughest for me to write while also very therapeutic— partly because it has been very challenging to receive a label for my "disease" and discuss it in a way others would understand. For the same reason, it is also one of the most important chapters, for perhaps it can help someone else put words to what they are going through. That said, in the descriptive stories that follow I speak only to my specific experiences, as they can look different for others. Let the vulnerability begin…

The stigma associated with mental health is slowly starting to decrease as more and more athletes, celebrities, and people of influence continue to open up about their struggles. I commend their bravery and willingness to share their difficult stories. Mental health disorders do not discriminate based on race, ethnicity, gender, socio-economic status, or intelligence – I am living proof of this. Many factors have played a role in my constant battle with mental health; however, I only consider myself a victim if I surrender control – and I'm not ready to do that.

While I have borne the brunt of the trauma directly on the field, it has lasted long after the game or season has ended; it has also bled into every aspect of my life. Family, friends, and doctors alike seem dumbfounded when I begin to describe what I'm going through. All too often I hear, "Jeff, you seem fine" or "I have trouble falling asleep at night too, Jeff."

But I'm not fine, and I'm just not like you. I have a brain disease, and I have accepted it. My inability to adequately communicate my struggles with others has made my life very challenging.

The loneliness I feel is debilitating. At times, I'm unable to get out of bed, leave the house, speak to anyone, go on a date, drive safely, sleep at all, have friendships, or relate with family. I feel an abnormal amount of frustration when adapting to my relationships with loved ones. My struggles look different from day to day. Some days, I act like a normal father, son, brother and uncle. The next day, I may be in a depressed state or forget the details of my interaction with them. My emotional and mental instability doesn't go unnoticed by my loved ones.

Most of the frustration lies with the fact that I don't completely under-stand my struggles, nor can I predict them. Some doctors, therapists, and counselors don't know anything about it. These unfortunate realities only add to my feelings of defeat and anger. This has left me questioning my life's purpose and if it was really worth living. The following poem, which I wrote in 2016, was inspired by these feelings.

"k-NO-w Purpose"
What purpose have I
Lingering between days
No alarm to set
Walls in my way.

What future have I
Without goal to obtain
No alarm to set
No progress to gain

What life have I
When no longer needed
No alarm to set
My mind…defeated

~Dec. 17, 2016

CRYING ON A FIRST DATE… AWKWARD (A Lighthearted "Break" Story)

Several years ago, for our first date, I took a woman out for dinner and a movie. I know, I know…movies on first dates are lame, but I really wanted to see that one, ha. So we sat down with our popcorn and looked forward to the main feature, *50/50* – which, by the way, was probably the *worst* movie to ever see on a date as it dealt with friendship and cancer. I realized this as the first preview played. As usual, the previews mirrored the same style as the featured attraction. During a particularly heart-felt preview, tears had begun to form and were running down my face, which did not go unnoticed by my date – and no, I never heard from her again. And I thought being a sensitive guy was a good thing! To make matters worse was that halfway through the movie, I realized that I had just seen *50/50* the week prior! (On a side note: I didn't remember how the movie ended either, so it was like seeing it for the first time, ha.)

CTE S*#T

Currently, Chronic Traumatic Encephalopathy (CTE) can only be definitively diagnosed after an individual is deceased. However, scientists are able to recognize signs and symptoms of this brain degeneration, which often don't begin to show themselves until years after the trauma has occurred. These traumatic brain injuries, which are endured by many athletes and non-athletes alike, present in many different ways. The symptoms can range from none at all, to mild or severe, and affect lives in varying degrees.

Fortunately, the NFL, top doctors and scientists are making great strides in the area of CTE. In the meantime, it is a constant challenge to explain it to my general practitioners, as well as to family, friends, and partners. I often hide my symptoms, cry when I can't recall things, and obsessively Google information in an effort to jog my memory.

MY GREATEST FEAR

People often ask me what the most difficult aspect of dealing with my "head issues" is. I must admit, I usually answer them in the simplest (and most dismissive) terms: "Sleep"; "Anxiety"; "Depression", et cetera. The real answer, of course, is not that simple. I have read every article and study I can find on CTE and degenerative brain disease, all with the same grim conclusion: the individual can be treated for their symptoms, but there is no cure. My greatest fear – losing my memory – seems to be occurring with increasing regularity.

It's hard to imagine living in a world where I don't recognize anything or anyone. I couldn't imagine not knowing what has happened earlier in my life. This ever-present obstacle leaves me with only one option-focus on delaying the process of degeneration as much as I can through treatment and pray that one day doctors may find a way to reverse it.

In the meantime, I must live in the present. I have accepted the terms of my disease. I have made adjustments to my daily life, I work with several therapists… but most of all, I'm trying to *live*. I could choose to merely exist or sit around and let my brain go to waste. Instead, I have chosen to address this obstacle with the same passion and dedication I had while playing in the NFL. Since currently this disease is not possible to overcome, I've found a way to go *around* it. I feel blessed in the present moment, in still being able to tell my story, and I trust that someone will benefit from it. My greatest fear isn't that I will die from CTE. It's that I'll stop living and be defeated before I'm able to make one last difference.

Glen Campbell was a musician/actor who saw success over the course of five decades, selling over forty-five million records worldwide. In 2011, he announced that he had been diagnosed with Alzheimer's disease. He passed away in 2017 at the age of eighty-one. In his final tour, he performed a song titled "I'm Not Gonna Miss You" that has impacted me a great deal. To me, the lyrics depict the later stages of Alzheimer's during which he would struggle to recall memories. Though he would not be "suffering," he knew that his loved ones would be. Like Mr. Campbell, I am concerned for my family and friends; I want them to know I'll be fine. I want my daughter to know I lived a great life and I lived it for her. It is my hope that my contribution to this world will remain long after my mental faculties are gone, just as his are.

"Let Me Forget to Remember"

I won't remember these words
I hope you remember my song

The grass isn't greener on my side
And the two things don't make a right

Each day is new or so I'm told
It'll all get better, just pull through

I get to live each day as if my first
As I'm unable to remember my last

All hands maintain my
            ...grip.

Please don't tell me that you know
Please go, but don't leave me alone

Love, peace and joy hide from me
Though I find myself, lacking them all

Please stay
      ...away
...from my pain.

~Jeff Ogden

FOREIGN THOUGHTS

"Do it with passion, or not at all."

~Rosa Nouchette Carey

As mentioned earlier, between my second and third years in the NFL the
Cowboys allocated me to NFL Europe. This league operated in the spring

during the off-season of the NFL and was designed to provide younger players with more game experience. This was particularly valuable for me as I was relatively new to playing the receiver position professionally. I made the most of this opportunity in the ten-game season. While that season provided many great memories, there was one incident in particular that I was unable to recall.

During the first few plays of a game versus the Berlin Thunder, I caught a short pass and ran up the sideline. A defender jumped on my back and tackled me on my way out of bounds. According to accounts and from watching the film, I know that I got to my feet and just stood there... on the *opponent's* sideline. Recognizing my inability to comprehend reality, the Berlin medical staff attended to me until I could be walked over to the appropriate sideline. Apparently, I then sat on the bench and just stared off into space.

The next thing I remember was walking with the team into the locker room at halftime...approximately an hour and a half later. At that point, we were losing 20-0. As always, the coaches asked me if I was able to go back into the game. As always I said yes – but there was one problem: I couldn't remember the plays. I had no idea where to line up or what route to run.

We received the kick-off to start the third quarter, trying to overcome a three-touchdown deficit. Our quarterback at the time was Heisman Trophy winner Danny Weurfel. Still suffering from the effects of my concussion, I relied on Danny for help. Upon breaking the huddle, he filled me on my individual responsibility. I was able to catch a few passes on that drive. He would later tell me that on the third pass, he was just throwing the ball to the ground to avoid a sack. Instead, I reached down, grabbed the ball with one hand, and outran the defender for a touchdown. Then, in a celebratory and uncharacteristic move, I threw the ball as far as I could up into the crowd before promptly falling to the ground and passing out, ha. I finished the game with two touchdowns and returned a kickoff for seventy-five yards which earned me Player of the Week honors; however, I only remember small snapshots of our 28-27 comeback victory.

"Really Me?"

Hauntings play behind my eyelids
Double features again and again

Momma's words, Jeffy, stay strong
Exhausted, Momma, of just hanging on

Papa points to his arm then his head
A behavior that keeps me undead

Experts diagnosed that I'm T&P
Please, My God, is this really me?

~ Jan. 13, 2018

TIMEOUT: Perfection is My Enemy

> *"You are imperfect, permanently and inevitably flawed. And you are beautiful."*
>
> ~Amy Bloom

As I look around at the world today, I am surrounded by the appearance of "perfection." It is very easy to view social media or read magazines and feel imperfect. This ideal of perfection appeared early on in my life as a gymnast. I obsessed with the tiny mistakes that kept the judges from awarding me that perfect score. This mentality carried over into my faith in God. I misinterpreted the power of sin and God's forgiveness, thinking that if I committed even the smallest indiscretion, I had let down God and He would be upset with me. I didn't allow myself to make mistakes, and if I did I would suffer severe guilt. I have since learned that my imperfections can lead to a more accurate assessment of who I truly am – and what I need to be the best version of myself – imperfections and all. God was cool with that too!

It is possible to bench press eight-hundred and eighty-five pounds (current World Record). Does bench pressing one hundred pounds mean you're not perfect?

CHALK TALK

Evaluate your time on social media/magazines. How much time do you spend on self-improvement? How can you accept yourself as perfectly imperfect? What steps would get you there?

> *"Perfections exist as moments in time, not as a product of time itself."*
>
> *~Jeff Ogden, high on coffee, 2021*

_____

_____

_____

_____

_____

_____

_____

_____

_____

_____

_____

_____

_____

_____

CAR ACCIDENT

Leading up to my car accident, which occurred a few years after retiring from the NFL, my life was very simple. My purpose was clear. I had no major obstacles to contend with. I had coached at the NFL, NFL European, College, and High School levels but decided to combine my love of education with my love of fitness in Pittsburgh, PA. I created a personal training business from my home but quickly outgrew that and opened my first gym just a few months later. Owning a gym was not satisfying enough. Individuals trying to lose five pounds for Spring Break or have bigger biceps just wasn't what I was passionate about. I wanted to provide a more in-depth, life-changing experience for clients. I wanted to train the body, heart, mind, and soul. I wanted to work with individuals and address every aspect of their life. So I decided to open a "wellness bed & breakfast." Here, clients would spend a week meeting with professionals from a variety of disciplines. Psychiatrists, yoga instructors, personal trainers, chefs, massage therapists, life coaches, and recreational guides would all contribute to the client's personalized program. I wanted to completely change lives and promote overall wellness.

Hidden Valley, Pennsylvania was the perfect location for this passion project. A beautiful community in the mountains about an hour outside Pittsburgh that attracts skiers during the winter and hikers and campers during the summer. There, I found and purchased a beautiful, spacious home to open my B&B. I was excited to create what I thought would be my life's work.

One day in August 2010, shortly before the closing date on my home, I finished up early at my gym and headed up to the resort to play golf. The leaves had already begun changing color, and as I drove up the mountain on the two-lane highway, I looked at the breathtaking scenery and became even more anxious for this new chapter of my life. That chapter, however, would be placed on immediate hold.

The accident happened in a fraction of a second but unfurled in slow motion, which is probably why I remember so many details about it. On this two-lane road, I recall two vehicles coming directly at me. One was on the proper side, the other was in my lane. The mountainside was to my left and a steep drop-off was to my immediate right. My eyes were fixated on the front grill of the oncoming SUV traveling around fifty-five miles an hour. My only recourse was to hit my brakes. I did so, then braced for impact with my arms pressing against the steering wheel. Boom. Later, I would learn that I left a ten-foot brake mark; the other driver never even tapped his breaks.

The first thing I remember following the collision was a man's voice telling me that everything was going to be okay and that the fire department would be there soon. Then the world faded to black. When I woke up again it was to the sound of sirens and metal splitting as the jaws-of-life stretched my SUV back out to its original length. Fade to black. Then I felt a medic's arms begin to pull me from my driver's seat, which was surrounded by the deployed airbags. "Watch my leg!" I screamed as I felt my right leg bend in places it wasn't designed to. I didn't know that the force of the impact and me braking had caused my right femur to snap and exit my right thigh. Fade to black. I also wasn't aware that my left arm was shattered, or that I had sustained a compound fracture in my foot. I blacked out yet again as I was transferred onto a stretcher and rushed to the "Life Flight" helicopter. The next time I came to, the EMTs began asking me questions. Surprisingly, I was able to answer coherently. I gave them the names of some friends they could call. We landed on the roof at the University of Pittsburgh Medical Center and they carefully placed my stretcher onto the concrete. "Careful with my leg!" I screamed again. Fade to black. I regained consciousness, this time in the operating room.

A few days later, I woke up in my hospital room, all smiles. I guess the morphine was doing its job, Ha. I told my family, who had flown in after getting word of the accident, and my girlfriend that I felt fine. It was no big deal, I said; this despite the fact that I had a catheter, breathing tubes, and morphine drip in my arm. The surgeons had placed a plate in my face by inserting it through my left eyelid. Another plate was inserted into my left forearm. My right femur had been tucked back in, along with a titanium rod, held in place by screws in my hip and knee. The surgeons had taken skin from my thigh to cover up the hole where my femur broke through. Oddly enough, no one believed me when I said I was fine (ha), but they humored me. They knew that soon enough, reality would set in.

VIEW FROM MY HOSPITAL BED

I had relied on my body to earn a scholarship, become a professional football player, promote fitness products, and open a gym. Now, in that split second, my body was shattered. After a two-week stay at the University of Pittsburgh Medical Center, I was sent home, where my living room had been transformed into a hospital ward. I would be confined to the bed for the duration of my healing process. Wheelchairs and walkers were not an option as I only had use of my right arm. My body was detoxing from the morphine drip I had coursing through my veins for two weeks. I stared out of my window, and my anxiety made me want to jump out of the window…only I couldn't even get out of bed to do that, ha. I had never been so sedentary, so trapped, or so physically helpless in my entire life. All that I had known, all that had provided me a living, was gone…or was it?

My body was not "gone" after the accident, but it was very different, with a lot of new hardware that had me feeling like the bionic man. My perspective, however, changed the most. I would come to realize that the tragic accident that had taken so much had also given me something invaluable: the knowledge that God had created me for more than just my physical abilities. His voice was never so clear to me during this time. I felt as though He had given me a wake-up call, a second chance. I had several months to do nothing other than evaluate my life. Had I been making the most of it? Had I been devoting my time to worthy causes? Had I placed proper value on family? I came to the conclusion that I hadn't. I chose to abandon my gym and wellness B&B and move closer to my daughter in Austin, Texas.

I had always thought that fighting for a roster spot with the Cowboys would be my greatest obstacle. It would turn out to be nothing compared to fighting for my life.

TIMEOUT: WHEN TRAGEDY STRIKES

I would be hard-pressed to meet someone who hasn't experienced any tragedies. Nothing – not even money, fame, or fortune – can protect us from events that negatively impact our lives. After making a living off my physical abilities, they were taken from me with a loud crash. Being diagnosed with a degenerative brain disease affects me to this day. My belief has always been that I could overcome any obstacle with hard work and effort. I have learned to accept tragic events. I know that while I may not be able to bust through every obstacle, there is always a way for me to climb over or move around them. An obstacle only becomes a wall if I let it stop me.

CHALK TALK

I know this is a sensitive topic and may be difficult to address. Have you experienced a hardship in your life? Have you grieved? Have you accepted it? How can this event (or events) strengthen you, build character, or improve values?

"To experience a tragedy and not grow from it, is a tragedy itself."

~ Me, 2021

A SEASON OF LOSS (THE DECLINE)

"I am no longer accepting the things I cannot change. I am changing the things I cannot accept."

~Angela Y. Davis

I began noticing some changes around six years ago. Back then, I, like the rest of the world, had no knowledge of CTE or Post-Concussion Syndrome. I just knew something wasn't "right" in my head. My behavior was abnormal. My cognitive function was declining rapidly. I didn't wake up one day and lose an ability. I didn't wake up and lose control of any faculty. Instead, signs and symptoms began presenting in a variety of ways, degrees, and times. They would appear gradually and, with time, increase in frequency and severity. An inability to sleep presented first and with extreme intensity.

At first, I attributed my insomnia to everything *other* than concussion issues. I would tell myself that I was too stressed out, taking on too much, worrying more than I should, et cetera. As time went on and my insomnia became worse. I felt it was time to seek medical help. I visited sleep doctors who would prescribe me the strongest sleep medications available. They would work for a night or two, but then seemed to have the opposite effect. Some sleepless nights brought disturbing hallucinations as well. Soon, the lack of sleep began affecting my work and life.

LOSING SLEEP

One of my many frustrations with the "insomnia" label is that everyone thinks that they have the cure: "Take melatonin"… "Try reading"… "Turn your TV off"… "Meditate"… "Drink warm milk." Someone even suggested that I wear a satin nightgown! (I'm not going to divulge whether or not I tried that one!) While good-intentioned, none of those things worked. I know, because I had tried everything. Well, not everything. Maybe I should shut off the TV and meditate while wearing a satin gown, holding a book in one hand and some melatonin and warm milk in the other?! Ha.

At that time, I was partnered with an outdoor fitness company. My work schedule required me to wake up at four-thirty a.m. to lead the five-thirty class. Before the insomnia, this had never been an issue for me. At first, when my sleeplessness set in, I would not sleep the Sunday before my Monday morning class. This progressed to not sleeping at all on Sunday or Monday night. (When I say "not sleeping" I mean I do not get a wink of sleep during the night, nor a nap during the day.) My struggles soon progressed to three or four consecutive nights without sleep and that's when I reached my breaking point. I remember driving to my classes in the morning and not being sure if I was awake or dreaming. I felt like I was floating through the world without really being present in it. The world felt like it was moving in slow motion; speech sounded like echoes, my body tingled at all times. Plainly stated, I was going crazy... and I knew it.

"Insomnia"
Staring at the clock, in hopes renewed
A silhouette of yesterday, no longer true

Slumber scares for what dreams may come
While darkness lingers, I pray for sun

This battle, a war that will never end
Unless this broken tree is able to bend

Fermented grapes, juice dulls the pain
Then showers seem but drizzling rain

I don't fear death, but agonize over the reality, the necessity of clinging to life."

~ Jeff Ogden, Dec. 17, 2016

LOSING MY MIND (The Story I Have Never Told)

Over the next year, my insomnia grew worse and worse, with no relief in sight. I fell into a deep depression. Although I had my dream job, my dream home in my dream city, amazing friends, and success, I was struggling to keep it together… to just hold on. With no medications helping, and scared that I was losing touch with reality, I checked myself into a psychiatric hospital. I was desperate to find some peace, some sleep, and most of all answers.

Upon my arrival, the admissions personnel asked me if I was suicidal. I responded, "I don't wanna die, but I can't and won't live like this anymore. Being conscious and alive is torturing me every day." Now, suicide is never the answer to any question, but at the time, in the state I was in, those feelings were true for me. The doctors gave me some potent medicine. I slept for sixteen hours the first night and twelve the second. I felt refreshed. That feeling didn't last. I wouldn't find my "solution" in the psychiatric hospital or the pills they prescribed that week, but that wouldn't prevent me from continuing to search. This obstacle would not write my story, nor finish it.

LOSING MY EXECUTIVE FUNCTION

My insomnia reappeared as soon as I left the hospital. I had no other option than to just "live with it," which was ironic because what I was doing could hardly be described as living. Then another issue began creeping its way into my life. I began noticing that I wasn't able to perform basic life tasks or functions. I would get what I called a "block" about certain things – I couldn't put a trash bag in the can; couldn't go to the mailbox; couldn't write checks; couldn't talk on the phone; couldn't read emails; couldn't read comments on social media posts. I was forced to employ others to perform these simple tasks for me. These and others continue to this day.

LOSING MY MEMORY

My deficiencies with my memory were easily explained away at the beginning. I developed strategies to hide my memory loss. Over time, though, my issues became more noticeable and more embarrassing. I would talk with someone one day and forget about it when I saw them the next. I would go to see a new movie, and then – as mentioned in my story about that first date – go back and see it the following week with no recollection of the first viewing. I hid a lot of these issues from everyone. When I did hint at my struggles, people were quick to respond that they "forget stuff all the time." Perhaps, but I doubt they had trouble remembering if a red light meant stop or go, something that happened to me often and made driving quite scary.

Other times, my friends and family would be speaking about a significant life experience and I would not recall any of it. I had also visited places, interacted with people and participated in activities that I could not recall at all. A common question people ask me is, "Do you remember when (fill in the blank)?" Sometimes I would lie and say that I did, but most of the time I had no idea what they were talking about. I spent many nights alone, crying over these unfortunate truths.

LOSING TO ANXIETY

Anxiety has been the most recent obstacle I've been working to overcome. In my previous professions, I did a lot of public speaking. I was in front of large groups leading fitness classes. I had no issues standing on stage in front of a church congregation or on the basketball floor at a high school assembly. That all changed two years ago. I found myself getting more anxious, more self-conscious, and overthinking everything. I began to lose my train of thought. I wasn't able to articulate my thoughts into words. I would experience an autonomic response of involuntarily sweating as I searched for the point of what I was saying.

Social conversations have been extremely challenging. Even today, I have difficulties listening to people speak, and then trying to process that information and develop an appropriate response. There may be a prolonged period of time before I'm able to respond. This has become pretty embarrassing and uncomfortable for both parties.

Of course, this has affected my dating/relationship life as well. I have avoided participating in this aspect of my life for fear of making a fool of myself. Telling a woman that I have a traumatic brain injury isn't the best "ice-breaker" on a first date, ha. I understand I am not "normal"; I have accepted that... but would a love interest? I feel hopeless just thinking about all the background information a potential partner would have to learn. I don't even completely understand myself and my issues yet, so how could someone else be okay with it all?

Anxiety has impacted and changed me in so many ways. It has prevented me from participating in my own life and the lives of my family and friends. Anxiety has triggered several full-blown panic attacks in public places. Traditional medicine has not been very effective, but I continue to work on techniques and coping mechanisms to help mitigate the effects of anxiety. I wear hats and sunglasses whenever I can just to feel hidden from the world.

I know this sounds silly, but to put this struggle into more clear terms, here are a couple examples. I began setting goals to leave my house each day. My gameplan for this is to only buy enough food for one dinner which forces me to go to the grocery store. This simple, daily occurrence is usually my only interaction with the public. I choose to hang out with friends and family only when they plan to stay in. Though I always intend to attend social events or go on dates, I usually cancel at the last minute. I am often lonely. I want to be a part of society and be actively involved in life. Instead, I am imprisoned by my anxiety and remain locked up in my home.

I have attempted to travel over the past few years. On one trip, I had to excuse myself from the security line as my breathing became shallow, my head began to sweat and I felt dizzy. In response to this and feeling desperate, I purchased a pass that allowed me to skip the long lines. It was expensive, but worth every penny to me. On another trip, as I was waiting at my gate to board the plane, I grew increasingly more paranoid. I felt that people were staring at me. I walked away and believed that fellow travelers were tracking my movements. I knew I was probably just imagining all of this, but I couldn't quite convince myself of that. Yet, despite all of this, I will continue to add daily goals and responsibilities in hopes that I may live and not just be alive.

LOSING CONNECTIONS

Sadly, I have not been the only one affected by the decline of my faculties. It has affected my family, friends, and loved ones as well. I gradually, and without fully realizing it, began distancing and isolating myself from all who cared about me. After several years of this practice, I found myself unable to have any type of dating life. I stopped hanging out with friends. I stopped answering my family's phone calls. This behavior led to agoraphobic tendencies as I avoided leaving my "cocoon" for any reason.

At this time, I did not understand what was "wrong" with me. Neither did most doctors. Information on the impacts of traumatic brain injuries as they relate to football was very limited. I was passed around to different medical specialists that treated each of my specific symptoms. Pills were prescribed to address them and hopefully allow me to resume a more normal life. At one point I was taking eight medications per day, yet none of them helped me approach a sense of normalcy. I am not faulting the doctors who previously treated me. They did not comprehend or have experience in treating the unique symptoms of football-related brain damage. As I mentioned earlier, the research is ongoing and in recent years progress has been made; I can only hope that it brings about effective treatments that are so desperately needed.

Being that I was ignorant of the reason for my behaviors, I did not know how to communicate them to others. I couldn't convey the overwhelming anxiety I felt while in social situations. I wasn't able to explain to a significant other why I lacked any emotion. I couldn't describe to my family the haze in my eyes when I saw the world in a skewed way. I found it difficult and embarrassing to cancel on my friends because I couldn't get out of bed, let alone leave my house. While all my relationships suffered, I felt more comfortable hiding from them rather than trying to explain my new and unwelcomed way of living.

Currently, my medications have been reduced. My diet has evolved to a more "brain-friendly" one which includes more vegetables, fish, nuts, and berries. I still struggle with the aforementioned behaviors but am able to communicate them without as much embarrassment. I am trying to be more accessible. I am not hiding. I am reconnecting with loved ones. I hope others who may be suffering from any one of these issues know that they, too, are not alone.

TIMEOUT: ME, MYSELF & I

I have learned that it's possible to be surrounded by friends, family, and loved ones and yet feel utterly alone. I have best described my feelings to doctors as, "It feels like torture to be conscious." Technically, I was alive, but the depression, insomnia, anxiety, agoraphobia, bipolar, and attention deficit disorder felt like anything but living. I was only existing…barely. The world saw me as a highly productive and successful contributor to society, but that wasn't an accurate representation of how I viewed myself. To me, I was just taking up space. Those feelings haven't vanished, but with the current breakthroughs and treatments from medical professionals, I now have hope.

CHALK TALK

Briefly write out a typical weekday and weekend: morning, afternoon and night. This may be hard to look at and may make you feel lonely. It makes me feel this way too. Are there any areas that seem imbalanced? Are you isolating yourself with video games, Netflix, drugs, alcohol, or social media? What healthy adjustments can be made? Are there any clubs/organizations that you could join? Any hobbies you'd like to try? Now, briefly write out an ideal day. Refer to this when you feel like isolating.

WHERE AM I NOW?

"Don't be a tomorrow person."

~FMCG

ave I defeated this disease? Have I delayed the onset of dementia or Alzheimer's? Have I learned how to once again become a contributing member of society? Have I successfully overcome the likelihood of CTE? No. These battles and struggles are ever-present, but the game's not over. There is still time left on the clock. I am learning to stop playing defense when battling this disease. I have taken a more offensive approach. I am quarterbacking my life and calling my own plays. I understand the need for conservative play-calls, but enjoy throwing the ball deep every once in a while!

THERAPEUTIC RECREATION

Having a body that feels like that of an eighty-eight-year-old man, I've had to find new outlets and new challenges for my desire to compete. Yes, you guessed it, I found Disc golf! Ha. Disc golf was a very foreign concept to me and I didn't quite understand why it is so popular, why ESPN has a TV deal with this sport, and why some of these athletes make millions of dollars. I soon found out why: it's addicting! I witnessed this new sport while beginning a hike. The athletes, yes I said athletes, were throwing discs hundreds of yards, weaving them through the trees, and competing with other athletes – all while they hiked from hole to hole. I wanted to try it, and after an initial investment of twenty-five dollars for the three essential discs (driver, mid-range, putter) I set out to dominate the course. It took me about seventy-five shots to finish nine holes when it would've taken a professional disc golfer around twenty shots. I guess I didn't dominate the course, but I was hooked. I didn't need a reservation, it was free to play, I got to hike, and most of all it provided a challenge. What I didn't expect was the therapeutic effect it had on my brain. I have found a way to refocus my desire to compete while not putting excessive strain on my mental well-being. Disc golf has been a much-needed, positive outlet for my life. I've been able to share it with my family and friends, who have experienced similar enjoyment.

Today disc golf can be found on YouTube (JomezPro) Disc Golf Network, and ESPN. There is also the Disc Golf Foundation, which aims to "grow the sport" in diverse communities, amongst children, and so on. I love all aspects of this form of therapeutic recreation. If disc golf isn't a "hole-in-one" for you (ha, ha) I would encourage you to find that hobby that evokes passion and fills your life with enjoyment.

Over the past couple of years, I have found purpose. I have found direction on my path. Writing a book was never a dream or goal of mine. In fact, it was probably the last thing I imagined myself doing. Now it has become both an outlet for me and a means of helping others, which, at the end of the day, *is* my ultimate dream.

TIMEOUT: DIS "ABLE"

Labels, Labels, Labels. We cannot escape them. They have become necessary for medical professionals to converse; they are a part of our day-to-day conversations. Unfortunately, these labels also have a tendency to define us and will continue to do so until we decide we will not allow it. Overcoming "labels" does not mean that diagnosis or conditions have disappeared. I have learned that I can take the power/control back by maximizing the abilities that I have at that moment. I still have goals and dreams…the road to them, however, is a little different than originally planned.

CHALK TALK

We have all been labeled at some point in our lives. How have you been labeled? Make a list of the labels you have been given from family, friends, teachers, coaches, colleagues, significant others, et cetera.

What labels have you placed on yourself to this point? Has your label defined you to this point? Now list five positive labels you'd like to have, i.e. loving, giving, strong, et cetera. Avoid things like "rich," "drives a certain car"; "has a big home"; "handsome"; "beautiful"; and so on.

If you are experiencing mental health challenges and/or suicidal thoughts, the following organizations can help:

National Suicide Prevention Lifeline
1-800-273-8255

Crisis Text Line
Text SILENCE 741741

Samhsa's Treatment Locator
1-800-662-4357

CONCLUSION

I hope that in telling my story – the good, the bad and the ugly – I have helped you realize that no matter what circumstances you are facing, you are not alone. That said, I also hope it helps you understand that at the end of the day we are all responsible for doing the work to overcome our obstacles, whether we have placed them in our own path or life did it for us. Below is a reminder in which you can further explore your answers to Chalk Talks, and hopefully is enjoyable too!

I, _____, have set goals to _____
(insert answers from the Timeout/Chalk Talk in the preseason section. My goals, which lay at the top of my staircase, are achievable through hard work and dedication. I am beginning to take intermediate steps to reach that summit. I will reward myself with _____
(input answers from the Timeout) when small victories occur.

I am so grateful to have an amazing support system, including _____(input names from the Timeout in the pre-season section). They are familiar with my goals and I will remember to lean on them for support and encouragement.

I understand that I will encounter obstacles on my journey, some of which will delay my progress or change my course. I will not consider these obstacles as failures and instead combat them by _____ (input answers from the First Half of the Introduction section). Not all my goals are attainable at the moment, such as, _____ (input answers from the Growth Mindset Timeout in the 2nd Half section). However, each day I will work on acquiring the necessary skills to push me toward the top of my staircase. Each day I will write out three tasks to accomplish, such as _____ (input answers from the Timeout in the 2nd Half section). This will keep me focused on the individual step ahead of me.

I am dedicated to tapping into my 212th degree and doing more than what is required of me. I know this practice will only aid me in taking the next step. Perfection is not necessary to achieve my goals, but I will _____ (input answers from the Time-out in the Off-Season section).

I no longer accept labels others have attributed to me and instead see myself as _____(input answers from the Timeout in the Off-Season section). Instead of doing what people think

I should be doing, I will focus on my own happiness, which includes
_____(input answers from the Timeout in the
Off-Season section).

I vow to love myself; take the stairs one step at a time; find ways around
obstacles and refrain from placing the following obstacles _____
_____ (insert answers from the Chalk
Talk in the Halftime section.). Most importantly, when faced with
uncertainty, I will tackle life head on!

ABOUT THE AUTHOR

Jeff was a former All-American at Eastern Washington University before his record-setting, five-year NFL career.

He walked-on to his alma mater after his brother, Pat convinced the coaching staff to give him a tryout. After developing in the program for three seasons, he became a NCAA Football Championship Subdivision All-America selection and First Team Academic All-American in 1997. Jeff earned a Bachelor of Arts degree in Special Education and Health Education.

"It was like watching a dandelion grow," said former Eastern head coach Mike Kramer. "Jeff had a pretty nondescript start to his career, but then he got better in the weight room... All of the sudden he became one of our most physically-gifted players ever."

He went on to play five years in the National Football League, starting with the Dallas Cowboys where he made the team as a rookie wide receiver/return specialist in 1998 as an undrafted free agent..

"I don't know what the expectations from the coaching staff were," said Hall-of-Fame quarterback Troy Aikman at the time. "But he worked hard and

he made some plays throughout the time we were in camp and the preseason games. He really caught everybody's attention and wound up making the squad."

Jeff also played in 1999 with the Cowboys before moving on to the Miami Dolphins (2000 and 2001) and Baltimore Ravens (2002). He had 28 career catches for 304 yards and a touchdown, had 57 punt returns, 15 kickoff returns and also played on kick coverage units. He set five records for the Dolphins – two in the regular season and three in the playoffs – and his 13.7 career average is still a franchise best.

During his professional career, he worked with the Fellowship of Christian Athletes and Athletes in Action. He also created his own foundation; *Jeff Ogden's Catch a Star Foundation*, which provided financial aid to prospective adoptive parents.

After retiring in 2003, Jeff pursued careers in education as well as owning his own fitness companies. He has left his fingerprints on many endeavors through his passion for life and tireless work ethic.

ACKNOWLEDGMENTS

To Momma, for demonstrating how to give one hundred percent of yourself to those you love. In my eyes, you're a Saint!

To Dad for always being in my corner and giving me confidence, and for the sacrifices you made so that I may live out my dreams.

To my brother, Pat, for pushing me to reach the potential I didn't know I had. I'm forever grateful for the doors you opened and the times you forcefully pushed me through them, ha.

To my sisters, Andrea and Janelle, for the memories we've created that we can never share with others...the laughter that ensued because of them... and the bonds that we have that can never be broken!

To my extended family: Dave and Samantha who have been there through the entire journey with loving support and words of wisdom. To my nieces and nephews, who were too young to remember or care, ha, but showed up in my team gear anyway: Mackenzie, Matt, Cali, Ruth, Nathan, Dumps, Maggie, Ella, Jacksen, and Lexi.

To JMC, for showing me doors, opening, and walking me through them.

-JDB, CMB, DD

R&PMcG.

To my coaches- TG, KG, DA, DZ, MK, RW, CG, JG2, DW, CU

Special thanks to my editor, Dana Micheli; my stylist, Nohemi O., my photographer, Nabor Godoy; and my publisher, Shanda Trofe of Transcendent Publishing.

Thank you, I love you all!

Made in the USA
Las Vegas, NV
31 December 2021

39868411R00095